THE
RHETORICAL
TRADITION
AND
MODERN WRITING

Edited by
JAMES J. MURPHY

THE MODERN LANGUAGE ASSOCIATION OF AMERICA
NEW YORK   1982

Richard E. Young's "Concepts of Art and the Teaching of Writing" is a revised version of an essay first published as "Arts, Crafts, Gifts, and Knacks: Some Disharmonies in the New Rhetoric," in *Reinventing the Rhetorical Tradition*, edited by Aviva Freedman and Ian Pringle (Ottawa: Canadian Council of Teachers of English, 1980), copyright by the Canadian Council of Teachers of English and reprinted in revised form by permission. The essay has also appeared in *Visible Language*, 14, No. 4 (1980), a special issue on "Dynamics of Writing" edited by Peter Wason.

Library of Congress Cataloging in Publication Data
Main entry under title:

The Rhetorical tradition and modern writing.

Includes bibliographical references and index.
Contents: Rhetorical history as a guide to the salvation of American reading and writing / James J. Murphy—Remarks on composition to the Yale English Department / E.D. Hirsch, Jr.—Restoring the humanities / James Kinneavy—[etc.]
1. English language—Rhetoric—Study and teaching (Higher)—Addresses, essays, lectures.
2. Rhetoric—History—Addresses, essays, lectures. I. Murphy, James Jerome.
PE1404.R5   808'.042'07073   82-2103
ISBN 0-87352-097-1   AACR2
ISBN 0-87352-098-X (pbk.)

Published by The Modern Language Association of America
62 Fifth Avenue, New York, New York 10011

Contents

Prologue   v

PART ONE: THE NEED

1. Rhetorical History as a Guide to the Salvation of American
   Reading and Writing: A Plea for Curricular Courage   3
   James J. Murphy

2. Remarks on Composition to the Yale English Department   13
   E. D. Hirsch, Jr.

3. Restoring the Humanities: The Return of Rhetoric from
   Exile   19
   James Kinneavy

PART TWO: HISTORICAL RHETORIC REAPPLIED

4. The *Phaedrus* Idyll as Ethical Play: The Platonic Stance 31
   Virginia N. Steinhoff

5. Classical Practice and Contemporary Basics   46
   Susan Miller

6. Ciceronian Rhetoric and the Rise of Science: The Plain Style
   Reconsidered   58
   S. Michael Halloran and Merrill D. Whitburn

7. John Locke's Contributions to Rhetoric   73
   Edward P. J. Corbett

8. Rhetoric in the Liberal Arts: Nineteenth-Century Scottish
   Universities   85
   Winifred Bryan Horner

9. Nineteenth-Century Psychology and the Shaping of Alexander
   Bain's *English Composition and Rhetoric*   95
   Gerald P. Mulderig

10. Three Nineteenth-Century Rhetoricians: The Humanist
    Alternative to Rhetoric as Skills Management   105
    Nan Johnson

11. Two Model Teachers and the Harvardization of English
    Departments   118
    Donald C. Stewart

12. Concepts of Art and the Teaching of Writing   130
    Richard E. Young

    Index   143

Prologue

We cannot understand what is happening unless we understand what happened. Furthermore, without a knowledge
of history, we have no way of knowing what is genuinely
new, what is redundant, what is promising, what has been
tried before and found wanting.

—RICHARD E. YOUNG

In a dozen different ways the writers presented in this book
all say the same thing—namely, that a knowledge of the rhetorical
past can help us solve the problems of writing in modern America.

Some of the essays draw lessons from individual teachers of
the past. Winifred Horner shows what can be learned from George
Jardine's efforts to design a writing curriculum for Scottish universities of the nineteenth century, which faced a situation much like that
faced by American universities today. Nan Johnson details the theories of Franz Theremin, Henry Day, and Matthew Hope as they
worked to restore a humanistic orientation to the teaching of composition and thus make it "communicative in substance and socially responsible in its aims." The popular *Manual* (1866) of Alexander Bain
is the subject of an essay by Gerald Mulderig that contrasts Bain's
association psychology, which aims to understand the mind of the
reader, with modern cognitive psychology, which strives instead to
understand the mind of the writer.

Two of the essays recommend books from the past that
might assist teachers in approaching their task. A thoughtful study
of Plato's *Phaedrus* by Virginia Steinhoff points to the "dialectical
enactment" involved in the activity of communication and provides
an illuminating contrast between the later influence of the speculative *Phaedrus* and the more easily schematized *Rhetoric* of Aristotle. E. P. J. Corbett argues that John Locke's *An Essay concerning
Human Understanding* (1690) offers teachers "insights into the human psyche that can enhance their teaching" and shows as well that
the *Essay* responds to all six issues identified by Wilbur S. Howell as
critical to the understanding of eighteenth-century rhetoric.

Specific teaching advice comes from two essays dealing with
ancient rhetoricians. A study of classical teaching methods leads Su-

san Miller to conclude that a modern teacher acquainted with the successful outcome of these methods will gain confidence in what she calls "unapologetic standards for successful student writing." The pedagogical advice of Quintilian in particular leads her to propose three practical principles for classroom use today. S. Michael Halloran and Merrill D. Whitburn argue that current thinking about "plain language" is rooted in the same simplistic positivism as were seventeenth-century views on the plain style, and they declare that "this positivistic view of the universe is even less appropriate in our own time than it was in the seventeenth century." In their view a much better model for the plain language movement can be found in classical thought on the plain style, particularly that of Cicero.

Donald C. Stewart analyzes the careers of two nineteenth-century American professors, Francis James Child and Fred Newton Scott, to demonstrate that university faculties have generally followed the Child model in what Stewart terms the "Harvardization" of English departments. "I still believe," Stewart writes, "that the profession of English . . . is out of adjustment with modern American society and that nothing could be more healthy for it now than a searching examination of its reasons for coming into being, its philosophies, and its heroes."

Addressing the Yale English faculty in a similar vein, E. D. Hirsch warns that certain issues keep recurring and that a faculty unaware of its own history faces a perilous situation. Those who know how and why writing and literature became separated are in a better position to make judgments about the future: "Then we can be sure that our profession will have returned to its authentic double vocation in literature and literacy." James J. Murphy calls for "curricular courage" among English departments so that they can use the lessons of history to reexamine what he calls the "three-tier system" of "literary" faculty, "creative writing" teachers, and composition "staff." The failure to engage in this painful self-analysis, he suggests, may result in the substitution of the microprocessor and autotutorial electronics for the human activity of reading and writing.

The Humanities in American Life, the 1980 report of the Commission on the Humanities, points to a decline in the role of the humanities in America. James Kinneavy responds by saying that "humanism needs a rhetorical component." His argument is that "possibly the single most telling reason for the decline of the humanities in the twentieth century has been the alienation of rhetoric from the humanities." The dramatic walkout of the speech and elocution members of English departments at the 1914 convention of the

Teachers of English was a further example of the fragmentation of language and discourse studies that the departmentalization of the nineteenth century had begun. The establishment of separate speech departments was another such step. "What we must do," he argues, "is to reintroduce into the various departments of the curriculum, but especially into the department of English, a concern for the persuasive as well as for the aesthetic and the scientific."

The final essay in this volume, Richard E. Young's "Concepts of Art and the Teaching of Writing," is placed last because the theories it discusses are the most recent. Starting with John Genung's *Practical Elements of Rhetoric* (1892), Young traces a number of twentieth-century approaches to the issue of "creativity" versus "mechanism" in the teaching of writing. He identifies a number of contemporary stances—the "new classicism," the "new romanticism," "heuristics," the "new rhetoric," "tagmemic rhetoric," and "the generative rhetoric of the sentence," among others—as current versions of a conflict over two concepts of art that can be traced to Gorgias, Plato, Aristotle, and Longinus. Behind this conflict, he suggests, there may be a conception of rhetorical art that does not force us to affirm one side at the cost of losing the value of the other.

In their various ways, then, each of these twelve essays challenges us to reexamine the way things are. Each argues that study of the rhetorical past can help us to analyze the present and to prepare for the future. The rhetorical tradition can thus be an informing element for the betterment of modern writing.

J.J.M.

PART ONE

The Need

1

Rhetorical History as a Guide to the Salvation of American Reading and Writing: A Plea for Curricular Courage

JAMES J. MURPHY

I

A famous lawyer, politician, and philosopher once complained that in his time there existed a ridiculous situation in which one set of teachers taught young men how to think, while a second set taught them how to use language. The complaint was made in the year 44 B.C. in a dialogue called *De Oratore;* the author was Marcus Tullius Cicero. Cicero blamed Socrates for the problem, but he was wrong. The problem lay in the educational establishment of his day.[1]

Now, two thousand years later, we face an equally ridiculous situation. One set of teachers is appointed to teach us how to read, while a second set tries to teach us how to write. We are in that situation at least partly because, like Cicero, we don't know our own history. Since we don't know our own history, we don't know whether we are making new discoveries or merely remaking old mistakes.

Consider American higher education, especially the 2,500-odd four-year institutions that help make American higher education one of the biggest businesses in the world. Virtually every one of them has an English department—even engineering schools have English departments—and in virtually every department there is a deeply rooted division between those who teach "reading," commonly called "literature," and those who teach "writing," commonly called "composition." This division is by now so deeply rooted in American colleges and universities that it affects the salaries and the prospects for tenure of those involved, the degree of respect accorded the two kinds of teachers, and probably such matters as who speaks to whom in the aisles of the local supermarket.

In more than a quarter century of interviewing job candidates, I have not seen a single recruit for the American army of English teachers who seemed to know how this situation came about. That is not surprising, for their graduate school mentors don't seem to know either. Everyone seems to accept the situation, as if it were always that way and must therefore always be that way. Ironically, the faculties of American colleges and universities seem to believe that their own English departments are a final product of some natural evolution, a sort of divine, immutable origin of the species as we now know it.

But English departments are a comparatively recent phenomenon. Take one example, that should be famous but is almost unknown to English professors. The history of the Boylston Professorship at Harvard University is virtually a paradigm of the history of English departments themselves. The first Professor was John Quincy Adams, who served from 1806 to 1809; the Harvard Corporation's detailed statutes charged him to instruct students in reading, writing, and speaking, using imitation and memorization as well as his own lectures. Basically, it was a program in classical rhetoric on the model of Quintilian. Later, Edward T. Channing (1819–51) was to include Whately's *Logic,* but he also began to include a concern for literature and for the "criticism" or evaluation of literature. When Francis James Child came to the chair in 1851, he brought a background in German scholarship acquired at Göttingen and especially an interest in criticism as opposed to composition, either oral or written. In 1876 Child was offered a professorship at the new Johns Hopkins University, the first American university founded on the German model of specialized scholarship. Child stayed at Harvard, but his title was changed to "Professor of English." In the same year, the Boylston Chair went to Adams Sherman Hill, who served until 1904. During that quarter century Harvard established a new department of English, and the old training in oratory gradually disappeared as class sizes mushroomed and "courses" under the "elective" system replaced the old concept of a single curriculum for all students. Thus the term "composition" at Harvard came to mean only written composition, and the term "rhetoric" was narrowed to mean only oral composition. In 1856 Edward T. Channing had said of rhetoric, "It does not ask whether a man is to be a speaker or a writer—a poet, philosopher, or debater, but simply—is it his wish to be put in the right way of communicating his mind with power to others, by words spoken or written." By the 1890s, however, a special committee of overseers at Harvard recommended that even written composition should be relegated to high schools.[2] What remained was "literature," in the sense of critical readings of acknowledged masterworks. Not surprisingly, a later holder of the Boylston Chair was the poet Archibald MacLeish.[3]

The Harvard example demonstrates that we might learn something about the present state of affairs by looking carefully at the issues of the past. Nevertheless, even the Harvard situation is but one instance of a much broader change in American attitudes toward rhetoric that took place over more than a century and is still only dimly understood today.

We need to know what has changed, why it changed, and whether we still wish to live with the results of that change. We must therefore learn our own history.

II

The first step in trying to understand the rhetorical tradition itself is to look back far enough in time to identify the elements of rhetoric before the comparatively recent changes in America.[4]

Ancient Greeks like Aristotle developed rhetoric as a theory of human communication—mainly oral—but it was the Romans who systematized it.[5] It was also the Romans who devised a coordinated teaching approach using reading, listening, writing, and speaking to teach rhetorical abilities on a mass scale. Schools followed the Roman armies throughout the empire, bringing literacy in Latin to the colonies from Britain to Asia Minor. In many places the schools survived the fall of the empire in A.D. 410. The enormous impact on Western civilization of the rhetorical tradition in Roman education in fact continued to influence the teaching of literacy everywhere in the West until at least the last century.[6]

The best single description of the ideal Roman rhetorical school may be found in the *Institutes of Oratory* (A.D. 95) by Marcus Fabius Quintilianus, which is perhaps the most influential single book on education yet published.[7] The methods described by Quintilian—the coordinated teaching of language through reading, speaking, listening, and writing—were employed throughout the Middle Ages even though the complete text of his book was not always available.[8] When Poggio Bracciolini rediscovered the complete text in the monastery at St. Gall, Switzerland, in 1416, the book electrified humanists. One friend wrote to Poggio, "Send me a copy so that I may see it before I die." The Italian example inspired English writers like Roger Ascham and Sir Thomas Elyot, so that by the time of

Queen Elizabeth Quintilian's educational methods were well established in English schools. Shakespeare as a schoolboy studied in a way that would have been familiar to Cicero, Seneca, Tacitus, Horace, and Vergil.[9] In the next century the poet John Milton did the same.[10] When, in Milton's century, the citizens of New Town on the Charles River in Massachusetts desired to open a school, they looked back to the only educational pattern they had known and brought masters from Cambridge University. The boys in the school to which John Harvard left part of his estate studied much the same way Shakespeare and Milton had, and much the same way boys had studied for the preceding millennium and a half.[11] Their regimen would have been familiar in principle to Quintilian.

What, then, is the program set forth by Quintilian that has proved to have so lasting a value? Throughout his training plan for boys, he insists that sight, sound, and sense be constantly interrelated and that the forms of prose and poetry be balanced against each other to provide variety for student exercises. At every stage the student first hears the master read or speak; then the student must speak, in paraphrase of or in response to what he has heard; then the student must write, first to imitate the form or style of what he has heard and read, then to "create" a version of his own; finally, he must read aloud what he has written, before both the master and his classmates. At times he must memorize it for recitation. He hears and sees his classmates do the same.

At first the material is simple—it might include the fables of Aesop—but the whole program depends on the systematic increase in the complexity of the material until after some years the student is working with actual laws or real histories. Ultimately, the student must master the *declamatio*, the composition and delivery of complete speeches as if he were already a lawyer or a senator.

At the heart of this Roman approach is the conviction that linguistic ability (*facilitas* is Quintilian's term) is a single, unitary human capacity, regardless of whether it is employed in reading or speaking or hearing or writing. Like a muscle, linguistic ability can be strengthened by purposefully stretching it into new uses, and, like a muscle, it can be reinforced by the repetition of varied uses. Thus, rewriting Greek prose into Latin verse exercises half a dozen specific abilities of form recognition and creativity.

Quintilian stresses the importance of listening, from the opening section of the book, where he urges that even infants' nurses be chosen with care for their speech: "It is they that the child will hear first; it is their words that he will try to form by imitation." He insists that education be "public," that is, in groups and not by private tutoring, for the students will learn by hearing one another and by hearing the advice of the master to those who make mistakes. "Writing makes speaking precise," Quintilian declares, "and speaking makes writing easy." Aristotle, in the first major ancient book on rhetoric, had written that rhetoric is a faculty that enables human beings to make the proper judgments about what to say in any given circumstance. Like Aristotle, Roman rhetoricians believed that this capacity (*facilitas*) could be applied to any form of expression, whether oral, written, facial, or bodily.

What of literature? It should not surprise us to discover that the study of what we would today call "literature" was an integral part of the Roman curriculum. For instance, Quintilian employs a definition of grammar that was commonly used until at least the fifteenth century: "Grammar is the art of speaking correctly, and of the interpretation of the poets." The *Iliad* and the *Odyssey* of Homer, as well as the works of contemporary poets like Horace and Vergil, could serve for "imitation" and study along with the writings of moralists, orators, and historians. This concern for literature is no mere concession on Quintilian's part, for a later part of his *Institutes* (Bks. X and XI) contains some of the most fervent defenses of the value of literature to be found anywhere in Western culture.

In one way or another, this coordinated curriculum for literacy—originally Roman but ultimately the warp and woof of Western education in general—lasted down into this century in Europe. In America it began to erode only in our parents' lifetime. Our ignorance of this change is a danger to our hopes for rational solutions to modern writing problems.

III

Thus, modern American teaching of both literature and composition has generally developed without faculty awareness of the Western cultural tradition that until this century had treated these two currently separated subjects as complementary modes of an integrated whole.

While there may have been some apparently good reasons for America's rejecting this tradition after World War I, it is certainly time to reexamine that peculiarly American decision. But who knows who made the decision or why it was made? This decision has resulted in the separation of reading from writing, creating a basically undemocratic situation that makes so-called literature an elitist, almost incomprehensible entity available only to the dogged survivors of boringly unrealistic classroom surveys, while creating a national aversion to writing, an aversion promoted by years of seemingly purposeless and rule-bound writing drills that have no apparent relation to human experiences in the real world.

This situation has created a national rhetorical vacuum. Citizens have now learned that reading is neither pleasant nor useful and that writing is both difficult and unnecessary. Some substitutes have stepped into this rhetorical vacuum—the telephone company, television, and now the electronic microchip. The term "word processor" now applies only to a machine, not to a human being. Do the faculty not realize that in this situation they are left to run only the schools but that the education of the citizenry goes on elsewhere, and in other ways?

Paradoxically, it is citizen awareness of the problem that makes this a uniquely valuable time to reassess the decision to separate writing from reading. The reintegration of human learning functions would be enormously popular (politically) and enormously satisfying (academically) if we only had the curricular courage to do it.

("Curricular courage" is perhaps an understatement. For one thing a painful restructuring of American university English departments would be required. The current three-tier organizational pattern would no doubt have to be collapsed into a single-level operation. In most places today there are three levels: the "literary" faculty of prestige and tenurability, the "creative writing" faculty of mixed antecedents and problematic futures, and the "composition *staff*" of the chronically underemployables of various stripes from teaching assistants to part-timers and the odd enthusiast from the so-called regular faculty. But, after all, isn't the term "creative writing" a redundancy? Show me a department with a thriving creative writing program, and I'll show you a department with a serious curricular disease—a detachment of the rhetorical retina. Any change in the now traditional hierarchy would be unpleasant to some and dangerous to others.)

What is needed, first of all, is the historical sense to realize that this separation of writing from reading was indeed brought about in America by conscious choice. That recognition requires a better sense of academic history than most people have today, so as a first step we must educate ourselves and our colleagues. Then, having identified what has got us into the current mess, we can decide how to make the reintegration of reading and writing that we abandoned earlier in this century.

This is not necessarily to say that we should bring back the teaching methods of ancient Greece and Rome or, least of all, the petty classroom drills of the nineteenth century.[12] But there were clearly some enduring principles of pedagogical integration that seemed to work well for many centuries and that we need to explore. Abraham Lincoln and Thomas Jefferson each had less formal education than either Gerald Ford or Jimmy Carter or Ronald Reagan. The answer, then, is not "more" but "better." The search for better education ought to begin with a clear historical sense of what worked so well for so long and what seemed to go wrong with that system to cause its rejection. We may well have thrown out the baby of literacy with the rhetorical bathwater.

We must reexamine a tradition that was effective for two thousand years and was abandoned in this country for a sort of Woolworth-level retail pragmatism—as many different salable composition approaches as the market would bear. The market now is angry with us retailers. Real pragmatism demands that we overhaul our delivery system, or we'll go the way of Chrysler and the British pound sterling.

It is therefore time to talk about our rhetorical sins, our two offenses against rhetorical morality. The first sin is abandonment. Somehow, teachers of composition in America—and this is, after all, mainly an American problem—have allowed writing to become isolated from the writer, from the rest of the curriculum, and from the orality and the reading that were its natural allies for two thousand years. The symptoms of this abandonment show up constantly in the journals, where an increasingly positivistic kind of experimentation has replaced intelligent empiricism. Process hunters and model makers have begun to replace teachers. No human being operates in the Flower-Hayes model, for example; instead, "the writer's long-term memory," which includes "stored writing plans," is at work. (Years ago Neal Postman complained that composition teachers were failing to get their students to ask the right questions, but how can a "long-term memory" ask a question anyway?) Man does not live by chi-squares alone.

The second sin is despair, a bewildered feeling that nothing can be done, a post-McLuhan inferiority complex. Elementary school teachers can't agree on any approach that will prepare students for the high school programs that university teachers blame for the writing problems they see. While we debate who is going to bale us out, the lifeboat sinks slowly under us. In a society in which jogging and dieting have become growth industries that have changed the habits of millions, we complain that Americans won't tolerate the learning of a discipline like composition. In a society in which a national championship marching band of 110 members comes from a school of only 350 pupils, we complain that modern students can't be motivated to do anything. It is better to light one small curriculum than to curse the Department of Education.

Of course it will be hard. It is always hard to stop and think.

To put it another way, this is the moral equivalent of World War II. The really successful industrial giants today are the ones who lost World War II, Germany and Japan. After 1945 both those countries had to start over, to rethink, and replan. I posit that American teachers of composition have unknowingly lost a war that they have deserved to lose. But no great Rhetorician-in-the-sky is going to come along with some Marshall Plan of a solution for us; we ourselves are going to have to do what Germany and Japan have had to do in the industrial sphere, that is, to start over, to rethink and replan.

We must look carefully at a proved, pragmatic, programmatic approach to the totality of the human experience involved in literacy. That programmatic approach was abandoned in America only in this century, in our parents' lifetime. Would it be impossible to rethink that approach in contemporary terms, to replan it for the 1980s and 1990s? It was the Romans, after all, who invented that apparently modern buzzword "process." Their term, borrowed from the Greeks, was *progymnasmata.*

Is this all just impractical antiquarian hogwash? Consider just one example of old principles reshaped to fit modern needs: when the internal combustion engine made motor cars possible, the cars used regular carriage wheels. The vibration ruined the delicately constructed engines, so Charles Goodyear invented the pneumatic tire to fit that ancient invention, the wheel. The wheel itself had worked for thousands of years, but the motorcar wheel had to be rethought and replanned to fit modern times.

We are all challenged to do two things. First, we must understand the principles involved in the programmatic, coordinated rhetorical system of teaching literacy explained by Quintilian and used for centuries in Europe and in America until about 1914. Second—a far harder thing rhetorically—we must make a modern adaptation work by convincing ourselves and our colleagues that a reexamination is the best plan for the 1980s and beyond.

We will need curricular courage of a high degree, for any realistic effort to recombine the shattered elements of human literacy at the college or university level will entail thinking the unthinkable. Some shocking questions will have to be asked: should we have dispensed with orality in English departments after speech departments split from them in the 1920s and the 1930s? should literature be used to teach writing? should listening skills be taught regularly? should teaching assistants be allowed to tamper with these delicate processes? should speaking exercises (oral composition) be coordinated with writing exercises (written composition)? If such questions are not asked on a national scale, we may find the alternative even less palatable.

The alternative is the kind of human programming that will, by default, substitute the microprocessor and autotutorial electronics for the human activity of writing and reading. Our failure will let Radio Shack design the curriculum, and Fred Silverman will be the dean. And that is a rhetorical World War III we cannot afford to lose.

To paraphrase an ancient Greek aphorism, those who do not study the history of rhetoric will be the victims of it. The first step we have to take into our future, then, is to look at our American past.

Notes

1 Cicero, *De Oratore*, trans. H. Rackham (Cambridge: Harvard Univ. Press, 1948), III.xvi.61; p. 49: "This is the source from which has sprung the undoubtedly absurd and unprofitable and reprehensible severance between the tongue and the brain, leading to or having one set of professors to teach us to think and another to teach us to speak."

2 Note for instance the admonitory tone of the title of the 1891 article by Byron S. Hurlburt, "The Preparatory Work in English as Seen by a Harvard Examiner," *Academy*, 6 (1891), 351–53.

3 For further details in this development see the essay by Donald C. Stewart elsewhere in this volume.

4 A useful annotated bibliography is that of Winifred B. Horner, ed., *Historical Rhetoric: An Annotated Bibliography of Selected Sources in English* (New York: Hall, 1980).

5 A useful survey of ancient rhetoric is provided by George A. Kennedy, *The Art of Persuasion in Greece* (Princeton: Princeton Univ. Press, 1963) and *Rhetoric in the Roman World* (Princeton: Princeton Univ. Press, 1972). Now also see the same author's *Classical Rhetoric and Its Christian and Secular Tradition from Ancient to Modern Times* (Chapel Hill: Univ. of North Carolina Press, 1980).

6 Lacking a sense of the history of how we use language, many observers fail to recognize some of these influences. For instance, most modern educators do not realize that the use of parallel structures in writing—now usually called a grammatical rule—was in Roman rhetoric merely a *recommendation* as an aid to climax. The California state written examination for teacher certification routinely includes examples of faulty parallelism for identification. Rhetorical practice, based on centuries of

teaching on the Roman model, has produced numerous rules of this kind in a number of modern languages.

[7] The pedagogical sections of Quintilian's *Institutio Oratoria* are published in *Quintilian on the Early Education of the Citizen-Orator*, trans. John Selby Watson and James J. Murphy, Library of Liberal Arts No. 220 (Indianapolis: Bobbs-Merrill, 1965). For a recent bibliography of works on Quintilian, see Keith V. Erickson, *Rhetoric Society Quarterly*, 11, No. 1 (1981), 45–62.

[8] See James J. Murphy, "The Teaching of Latin as a Foreign Language in the Twelfth Century," *Historiographia Linguistica*, 11 (1980), 159–75. About 1344 the faculty of Grammar at Oxford University issued instructions to teachers that would surely have pleased Quintilian; note the correlation of sound, style, and memory:

> Every fortnight they [i.e., the students] must present verses and compositions (*literas*), put together with fitting words, not swollen or half a yard long, and with *clausulae* concise and appropriate displaying metaphors, and, as much as possible, replete with *sententiae;* which verses and compositions, those who are given the task should write on parchment on the next free day or before, and then on the following day when they return to school they must recite them by heart to the master, and hand in their writings. Henry Anstey, ed., *Monumenta Academica Oxoniensis*, 2 vols. (London, 1868) II, 437–38.

[9] T. W. Baldwin, *William Shakespeare's Small Latine and Lesse Greeke*, 2 vols. (Champaign: Univ. of Illinois Press, 1944). A reader may gain some sense of the pervasive nature of rhetoric in this period through an examination of the more than 800 authors listed in James J. Murphy, *Renaissance Rhetoric: A Short-Title Catalogue ... with a Select Basic Bibliography of Secondary Works* (New York: Garland, 1981).

[10] Donald Lemen Clark, *John Milton at St. Paul's School: A Study of Ancient Rhetoric in English Renaissance Education* (New York: Columbia Univ. Press, 1948).

[11] It is interesting to note that the description of the first Harvard College commencement (in 1642) is very close to that of William Fitzstephen's description of public exercises in oratory, disputation, and verse writing at St. Paul's School, London (in 1170).

[12] A famous example of methods to be avoided, of course, is to be found in Thomas Hughes, *Tom Brown's School Days* (London, 1857).

2

Remarks on Composition to the Yale English Department*

E. D. HIRSCH, JR.

What can I say about composition that will be useful to the Yale English department in setting up a good writing program? It's clear to me that I won't need to say anything about special teaching methods that are tailor-made for the Yale scene. Yale's admissions policy guarantees that entering freshmen are going to be very diverse in their backgrounds and in their writing skills, and Yale will want to adapt to this diversity by using methods that are flexible and eclectic. Even if Yale did try to create a novel program that could serve as a model for the rest of the nation, it's doubtful that the elements of the program could be new or that the human mind could devise more methods and programs than have already been tried out. The problem will be to choose methods intelligently and to apply them well; and in order to do this, the one thing needful is not machinery but motivation—professorial motivation.

As you know, present-day students do not need to be motivated; they are eager to learn how to write well. In every college I know of, students are flooding into writing courses, especially into those labeled "advanced writing" or "technical writing" or "creative writing" or "news writing" or the like—all of which teach essentially the same skills. Students want to take these courses. Many applicants have to be turned away even though we are increasing the number of courses every year. Our principal task is to make these courses first-rate, and that is, as I said, a matter of professorial motivation. At Yale, as at every other good college in the nation, the composition problem is largely a problem of professorial neglect. That must be the realization behind this attention-getting symposium. The antidote to neglect is attention, and as English teachers we need to find enough intrinsic interest in the subject of composition to hold our attention even after the current literacy panic has run its course.

For anyone in my own generation, the fact of professorial neglect does not have to be documented in detail. In my own experience, I see the pattern of the whole. In my first year as a college English teacher—that was at Yale in 1957—I was naturally assigned 8:00 a.m. freshman classes, as was appropriate for the juniormost instructor. But in all my years at Yale, I was never assigned a composition course. I was told that there existed a few sections of something called "Bonehead English," but I never saw a syllabus of the course or met anyone who admitted teaching the course. One simply did not own up to getting such a teaching assignment in those days. My first composition course came over a decade later, in 1969, when I was a department chairman at the University of Virginia and I thought it might boost morale if I taught a composition section. That teaching experience was decisive for me in a number of ways, all springing from the realization that I was doing a terrible job of teaching composition. I saw that we should reorient our values at Virginia and that we should certainly train our composition teachers better than I had been trained.

So much for reminiscence. To some degree my personal experience documents the general, but by no means universal, neglect into which composition has fallen over the past twenty-five or thirty years. But I think it is important to understand that these past three decades have been an unnatural and anomalous period in the history of our profession. The conditions in which we were trained were unnatural conditions, and the state of English studies that we now take for granted did not exist before 1950 and may never exist again. It's probable that we are now at the end of a unique era in the history of English studies.

I've dated the beginning of that era at about 1950. It is no accident that this date marked the founding of the 4-Cs organization, the Conference on College Composition and Communication. It's no accident, because just about then literary studies were widely declaring their autonomy as a discipline. If on one side the watchword was the literary study of literature, then the utilitarian study of composition was naturally what was left for the other side. It was equally natural that our profession should divide itself into two classes—antiutilitarian literary elite and an underpaid coolie class who labored in the fields of composition. The founding of the 4-Cs and the dominance of the literary study of literature were related, simultaneous events.

This fall into disunity has always been a moral danger for our profession, which from its earliest days comprised a two-sided interest in literature and literacy. Our profession began in the late eighteenth century with the advent of mass literacy and mass education. Before that, as you know, a literary education was an education in the ancient classics. University professors of vernacular literature began to be appointed only when literacy began to be widespread. The intimate connection of our profession with mass literacy is quite evident in the interesting fact that the first English professor was not an Englishman but a Scotsman, for whereas the English people of the eighteenth century were not very literate, the Scots could boast the highest literacy rate in Europe. Accordingly, the first chair in our profession was endowed in 1762, at a Scottish university—the University of Edinburgh. The title of this first chair also has a highly significant connection with literacy: "Professor of Rhetoric and Belles Lettres," which translates into current terms as "Professor of Composition and Literature." The first occupant of this composite chair was Hugh Blair, whose lectures on rhetoric remained a standard composition textbook for many decades.

The logic of giving Blair's professorship a double title lay in the conscious cultural connection that the Scots drew between literacy in vernacular language skills and literacy in the vernacular cultural tradition. The two kinds of literacy were deliberately fostered as a democratic equivalent to a classical education. From the very beginning, the English professor was therefore an agent of a democratic, universal education as opposed to an aristocratic, elitist education. Hence, it was inherent in the very concept of our profession that an English professor should be a teacher of literacy as well as a teacher of literature—the two sides of the job supporting and validating each other.

Although this tradition has prevailed until the recent past, our composite profession has always faced the danger of a collapse into separation and disunity throughout its two hundred years of existence. In fact, more than a hundred years after the founding of the Edinburgh chair, Edward Dowden, the distinguished scholar of Shakespeare and biographer of Shelley, was warning his Victorian contemporaries against one-sided belletrism (Dowden's chair, by the way, had the appropriately composite title "Professor of Oratory and English Literature"):

> While the study of literature may have something to fear on the one side from the science of philology which threatens to usurp its place and name, it views with alarm on the other hand what I may name the belles lettres heresy. The study of literature—English or other—is not a study solely of what is graceful, attractive and pleasure giving in books.

Dowden, like Newman, believed in a balance between the literary study of literature and the larger scope of literate and even utilitarian education. It was the same kind of balance that Matthew Arnold consistently advocated in education and culture. The most distinguished Victorian professors of English saw the danger of one-sided aestheticism and they avoided it. In the United States, we too avoided the fall into belletristic one-sidedness until about 1950.

That was the year of my graduation from an Ivy League college—Cornell. Four years earlier, as a freshman in that institution, I was required to take a full year of composition and was lucky enough to have as my instructor Professor William Sale, who was not only chairman of the English department and a distinguished scholar in eighteenth-century literature but also coauthor of our composition textbook. That was the kind of pattern that persisted in the Ivy League until about 1950, and it still persists, of course, in many colleges. Cornell is now returning to the earlier pattern, and if Yale is going to do the same, we can be sure that our recent experiment at being exclusively professors of literature has been a rather short-lived and unsuccessful one, with unfortunate practical consequences. Let me repeat: in the past thirty years we English professors have been living through an unnatural, uncharacteristic, and unhealthy period of disconnection from the roots of literacy in our historically composite profession.

These observations suggest that a historical adjustment is overdue and is now in the making. Yale, as a leader in English studies, has an opportunity to take a leading role in that historical adjustment, instead of fighting a rearguard action against it. Yale could begin to do a great deal more than foster good instruction in undergraduate writing courses, though that is of course the duty that needs to be met first. Yale could also take the lead by restoring in its Ph.D. program the historical connection between the teaching of literature and the teaching of literacy. If it makes that adjustment, the quality of instruction in its writing courses should automatically rise rapidly. A rather painless adjustment in the Ph.D. program would help significantly in fostering the larger historical adjustment that we need.

My suggestion is this: a Yale Ph.D. in English should guarantee expertness not just in literature but in literacy as well. Since the structure of the American English department is unlikely to change very quickly, a doctorate in English should still certify expertness in a historical period of literature. But because we are also teachers of literacy, a doctorate should also certify expertise in the teaching of writing. Moreover, since the research frontiers in literacy are significant and exciting, a Yale doctoral program in English ought to permit research specialization and a dissertation in literacy. A candidate who does research in literacy should still demonstrate expertness in a literary specialty. Similarly, if the special research is in literature, the candidate should demonstrate a theoretical and practical knowledge of composition. In short, a good Ph.D. program in English ought to reflect the composite character of our profession and turn out professors of rhetoric *and* belles lettres, as in the days of yore.

Now I'll quickly leave this practical suggestion about what Yale might do in its Ph.D. program to improve the teaching of writing. In the long run, such an adjustment in the Yale Ph.D. would be tremendously beneficial to the rest of the country. But in the short run, I see the main problem at Yale as one of reorientation of professorial motivation. So I want to conclude my brief remarks on a note that appeals to Yale's tradition of leadership and idealism.

We know about the current outcry for minimal-competency tests in writing. These writing tests are going to affect hundreds of thousands, indeed millions, of people and will determine the character of English teaching for many years to come. In New York State, for instance, after 1980, students will receive high school diplomas only if they pass a writing test that requires three separate short compositions on assigned topics. But who are the experts who are deciding on the aims and characteristics of these writing tests? It is by the merest accident that I was appointed to the national Advisory Panel for the New York State tests. I was not invited because I was an English professor in a good English department or because I had written a theoretical book on composition. I was invited only because I have been doing research on the scoring of writing tests, and my special knowledge was needed. Otherwise, I would have been considered an irrelevancy in these days of the literary study of literature. This committee is making decisions that not only will determine what is done in New York State but, by an arrangement with the College Board, may influence what is done throughout the country. It is therefore a committee that wields more power for good or ill in the teaching of English than any other committee that I know of. Forty years ago, the chairman of the New York Regents National Advisory Committee would probably have been the chairman of the Yale English department—someone like Edward Dowden or Matthew Arnold. His colleagues would have been first-class literary scholars as well as scholars in literacy. Today, such a group could not even be assembled. It is a great loss to ourselves and to our culture that our literary profession has cut itself off in this way from the other half of our vocation. I shall conclude by looking forward to a time when such a powerful committee is headed by the chairman of the Yale English department. Then we can be sure that our profession will have returned to its authentic double vocation in literature and literacy. When that time does come round again, there won't be any need for symposia like this one on how to teach writing to Yale undergraduates.

Note

* Reprinted from *The State of the Discipline, 1970s–1980s*, a special issue of the *ADE Bulletin*, No. 62 (1979), pp. 63–65.

3

Restoring the Humanities: The Return of Rhetoric from Exile

JAMES L. KINNEAVY

The recent publication of *The Humanities in American Life*, the Report of the Commission on the Humanities,[1] cannot but cause anyone interested in the present or future of the humanities to be concerned. The report is a careful survey of the status of the humanities in the schools, in higher education, in communities, and in private life. Each section includes a series of recommendations, all attempting to improve the lot of the humanities in the 1980s.

The survey of the status of the humanities in America is thorough and the recommendations are timely and important. Nonetheless, the report is disheartening. As the report says, "We proceed from the premise that the humanities are widely undervalued and often poorly understood." Indeed, it was this "profound disquiet about the humanities in our culture" that initially prompted the formation of the commission (pp. 4, xi). The same concern motivated the report of a similar commission in 1964.[2] The current report's chapter on the high schools and elementary schools is particularly discouraging (*Humanities in American Life*, pp. 25–59).

After reading these chapters, a pensive reviewer has to ask two critical questions: (1) Why have the humanities declined so markedly in the schools *and* in the colleges? and (2) How can the decline be reversed? Instead of attempting broad and multiple answers to these queries, I would like to focus on one area common to the responses to both questions.

Neither of the reports can be viewed as a history, that is, a causal inquiry into changes in the status of the humanities from one age to another. Yet both reports chronicle the decline of the humanities.

Possibly the single most telling reason for the decline of the humanities in the twentieth century has been the alienation of rhetoric from the humanities. Conversely, one of the most promising saviors of the humanities might be the restoration of rhetoric to the humanities in our schools and colleges and eventually in the populace at large. This is a pretentious proposition, I admit, for anyone to defend in the confines of a small article in an anthology on the history of rhetoric. Let me at least indicate the outline a defense might take.

The sketch of the defense must first include some historical rationale for the decline of rhetoric in the humanities and their resulting disfavor. Second, the defense should indicate the restorative effects the reentry of rhetoric into the schools and colleges might accomplish.

To avoid misunderstandings, allow me a stipulative definition of rhetoric. In this context, I mean by "rhetoric" the kind of discourse that is exemplified by political speeches, legal persuasion in court, religious sermons, commercial advertising, etc. I do not include in rhetoric most scientific writing, fictitious or poetic writing, or even informative news stories. In other words, I limit "rhetoric" to the meaning it had in the trilogy of the traditional liberal arts of grammar (literature), rhetoric, and logic. This delineation gives at least some historical realism to the definition. There may of course be major overlappings among these three kinds of discourse, but overlappings do not constitute a serious enough reason to repudiate the general validity of the basic taxonomy. In a color spectrum, some blue and violet may overlap, but this fact does not obviate the usefulness of distinguishing blue from violet as distinct colors.

Now, I maintain that for 2,100 years the study and the production of persuasion (as defined above) formed the core of the humanities and linked the humanities to the practical life of the everyday citizen. Rhetoric, in other words, made the humanities relevant to the political and religious life of society. Because they no longer constitute this core and this vital link, the humanities have, not surprisingly, lost some of their allure.

It is a bald historical fact that the humanities were born in a rhetorical manger. The first recorded use of the word *humanitas* is in the *Rhetorica ad Herrenium*, a text roughly contemporaneous with Cicero. Its Greek equivalent, *anthropismos*, first appears in the work of a sophist rhetorician named Aristippus, who gave the notion its intellectual dimension.[3] The Greeks, however, did not use this term or the alternative *philanthropia* in as general a sense as the Romans used *humanitas*. The more general term that unified the notions of the humanities was the cluster term "freedom" (*eleutheria*).[4] The rhetorical origins of these two terms will be discussed immediately below.

More important than these terms are the ideas of the two

persons most responsible for the tradition of the humanities in Western civilization, Isocrates and Cicero. Historians like Jaeger—somewhat grudgingly—and Marrou, Hadas, Snell, and others—much more enthusiastically—acknowledge Isocrates as the father of humanism.[5]

The bases on which Isocrates constructed his concept of humanity were several very practical concerns in Greek life. One was the Athenian notion of a guest's right to protection and compassion, a favorite theme of the tragedians, reiterated frequently by the historians and rhetoricians and by Isocrates himself.[6] This notion was an element of a larger concept that stressed the importance of being a social group bound by laws. Odysseus speaks disparagingly of the Cyclops to King Alcinous, the ruler of the Phaeacians:

> They have no laws nor assemblies of the people, but live in caves on the tops of high mountains; each is lord and master in his family, and they take no account of their neighbors.[7]

Isocrates takes these two practical concerns and enlarges them into the notion of social welfare, which, as Wehrli has indicated, is the essence of the idea of humanity (pp. 7–14). Since the implementation of such a program by laws and assemblies presupposes individuals speaking freely in a society, the conceptions of freedom, free speech, the city (the Greek social entity), and an individual's right to make decisions were necessary axioms of the system. The system was concerned with the care of neighbors or even strangers. Isocrates made it quite clear that the instrument for persuading the city assembly to adopt laws was the power of persuasion by speech—in a word, rhetoric. Rhetoric was thus the basis of all culture and civilization.[8] Isocrates' humanism was unabashedly rhetorical (not literary, not scientific) and was linked to the practical world of politics, particularly Panhellenism.

To train citizens to be persuasive in a political environment, the environment of the *polis*, the education of children and of young men was required. Consequently, for Isocrates and for the ancient Greeks generally, education, free speech, and compassion for one's neighbor and the notion of the city were all interrelated concepts, usually unified under the central notion of freedom (Wehrli, p. 13). To achieve this education, Isocrates insisted on a canonical list of readings in history and literature (Hadas, p. 129). In emphasizing that the enterprise of persuasion was carried out by the free decisions of individuals, without the assistance of the gods, Isocrates was following Protagoras and other sophists. In fact, in most Greek drama, men and women make their own decisions.[9]

The extension of compassion for one's neighbor to compassion for all human beings seems first to have been made by Euripides in the *Medea.*[10] Isocrates extends the notion of the geographical Greek to that of the intellectual Greek (that is, one who is educated) in a famous passage in the *Panegyricus:*

> And so far has our city distanced the rest of mankind in thought and in speech that her pupils have become the teachers of the rest of the world; and she has brought it about that the name "Hellenes" suggests no longer a race but an intelligence, and that the title "Hellenes" is applied rather to those who share our culture than to those who share a common blood.[11]

This oft-cited and controversial passage is used by Jaeger, among others, to show that Isocrates equates Panhellenism with education and the barbarians with the noneducated.[12]

Isocrates' humanism, finally, was consciously practical and opposed to the theoretical and the speculative. In the controversy between the advocates of *theoria* and *praxis* in Greek education, Isocrates was possibly the most influential figure in determining the thrust of subsequent *paideia* toward the practical, especially toward rhetoric. In fact, according to Gauthier and Jolif, it was the powerful influence of Isocrates that made even Plato change his position in the latter part of his life and that made Aristotle turn from his early Platonic position to the practicality of his later work.[13] Plato had inveighed against the practical kind of knowledge exhibited by Themistocles and Pericles in the *Gorgias* and the *Meno;* Isocrates takes these two and holds them up as examples of his type of intellectual hero.[14]

This practical, politically oriented notion of humanism, with rhetoric at its core, was taken over by Cicero. He refined it and passed it on to the Middle Ages and the Renaissance. In his early rhetorical treatise *De Inventione,* he became the first to use the term *artes liberales,* although Aristotle had addressed himself to the concept. In Cicero and in Aristotle, the phrase existed in a political context, a fact that Newman tends to forget in his handling of the disinterested nature of university education in "Knowledge Its Own End" in *The Idea of a University.*[15]

This rhetorical core, championed by Isocrates and Cicero, was the educational focus for humanism and education in antiquity, the Middle Ages, and the Renaissance. It was translated into pedagogical practice in the most influential and enduring set of textbooks in the history of Western civilization, the rhetorical exercises called the *progymnasmata.* These exercises prepared students to make full-scale legal and political speeches by introducing them to a series of persuasive types of writing ranging from narratives, proverb exempla, and descriptions to confirmations, confutations, impersonations, and proposed legislation.[16] The exercises, popular throughout antiquity, the Middle Ages, and the Renaissance in the Byzantine East and the European West, provided the rhetorical backbone of the humanistic tradition in the classrooms of our civilization.

The legal, political, and religious content of the exercises supplied students with a practical link to their lives. It is this practical link that I miss in the humanities as they are conceived today. Even the tolerant view of the humanities espoused in the 1980 report of the commission does not really advert to the rhetorical core of the tradition. It includes language and literature; but "language" nearly always signifies either linguistics or foreign languages and "literature" usually means belletristic fiction, poetry, and drama.

No one has written the history of the progressive alienation of rhetoric from the humanistic tradition, an alienation that probably began with the anti-Ciceronians in the sixteenth century and flourished with the antirhetoricians of the Royal Society in England in the seventeenth century and with the rise of journalism and the revolt against rhetorical topics in the eighteenth century. The disinterested nature of humanistic education, as championed by Newman and others in the celebrated disputes between the advocates of liberal education and professional preparation in the nineteenth century, probably also contributed to the decline of the hegemony of rhetoric in the humanities and, consequently, to a decline in their practical orientation. Finally, the departmentalization of disciplines in universities in the nineteenth and twentieth centuries seriously affected rhetoric.

In America departmentalization gave rise to the melodramatic walkout of the speech and elocution members of English departments at the 1914 convention of the National Council of Teachers of English. These dissidents took rhetoric and debate with them to the new departments of speech. Henceforth, in America at least, rhetoric was not a required course in the educational sequence. A similar direction was taken at about the same time by logic, which went to the departments of philosophy or mathematics. These secessions made the English department, with its courses in literature and language (philology), the sole inheritor of the full liberal arts tradition. Unfortunately, the teachers and scholars in the new departments of English were not given any rhetorical training or any preparation in systematic logic, either traditional or modern.

As a result of these departures, English departments were left with two functions: studying belletristic literature and studying language structures and history. Studying belletristic literature often consisted of writing analytical themes about literature, but the tradition of writing persuasive themes relevant to the daily political, legal, or religious life of the student was lost. The orientation of English departments was similar to that of the humanities generally. The humanities became more belletristic, more concerned with the fine arts or with history and expository discourse, but less and less concerned with rhetoric.

Such a move explains why I had to write a two-page justification for including rhetoric in a proposal to the Texas Council for the Humanities last year. It explains the progressive exclusion of essayists from the twentieth-century canon of literary writers in current textbooks and anthologies of literature. It partially explains the popularity and pervasive influence of the New Criticism, as well as the current popularity of the semiological as opposed to the semantic approach to literature (the semantic approach relates literature to the outside world, the semiological approach is interested only in the internal structures of the work of art).[17]

These trends make the humanities seem less relevant to the ordinary person, to school boards, to state departments of education, and to the student selecting courses from a college catalog. To counteract them I propose that we take a lesson from the history of the humanistic tradition: humanism needs a rhetorical component. It is this component that most effectively relates humanism to the daily lives of the average American citizen. Kierkegaard recognized the commitment involved in rhetoric, which he found absent in the more neutral discourses of literature and science.[18] Literature and science can be disengaged and disinterested—Newman and Kierkegaard, for all of their differences, agree on this. But rhetoric—religious for both Newman and Kierkegaard—requires a commitment. Unfortunately, our high schools and colleges recognize the validity of expository prose in science and in reportorial journalism and of creative writing in fiction and poetry, but they usually frown on the persuasive prose of rhetoric. Only departments of religion, advertising, and journalism (in editorial writing) give the student an opportunity to indulge in engaged prose. Unfortunately, with the exception of journalism, these departments are absent in the high schools, and high school journalism courses reach only a minute portion of the student body. In other words, only a small percentage of high school or college students ever systematically learns persuasive prose or ever analyzes it.

We must reintroduce into the various departments of the curriculum, but especially into the department of English, a concern for the persuasive as well as for the aesthetic and the scientific. We need not neglect the literary or the scientific—far from it—but we must address the three concerns somewhere in the curriculum. Rhetoric never excluded the aesthetic or the scientific or the dialectical, even in ancient Greece. Indeed, archaeological findings confirm that Homer was the primary source of instruction throughout Greek history. In a listing of early literary papyri, Oldfather shows that the *Iliad* accounted for half of all the holdings and that the *Odyssey* was second in importance, followed by Demosthenes, Euripides, Menander, Plato, Thucydides, Xenophon, Isocrates, Pindar, Sophocles, Aristophanes, Sappho, Theocritus, and Bacchylides.[19] According to Martial, the most popular authors in Rome were Homer, Vergil, Cicero, Livy, and Ovid.[20] What is noteworthy in these listings is the presence, in both Greece and Rome, of orators and rhetoricians.

The reintroduction of rhetoric into the curriculum would entail both a production and an analysis dimension. In the production dimension, students would write prose that exploited the emotions of the audience through personal voice and feelings, using style as well as logic and information. Such a program would return to the kinds of themes represented by the *progymnasmata*, or elementary exercises, as Donald Lemen Clark translates the term (Clark, pp. 177–211). It would mean that departments of history, anthropology, government, physics, chemistry, social work, and so on would allow their students to write prose, even impassioned prose, about the issues of these disciplines. Such a suggestion would indeed give a new dimension to the recommendation of the report on writing in different disciplines. Nearly all the writing in such departments is currently restricted to expository or informative prose.

While students in English departments in both high school and college should continue to write themes that analyze literary masterpieces, they should also write persuasive themes on current topics of political or educational interest or on topics of interest to the individual student. Such topics are not routinely assigned in typical English departments today. In fact, literary analysis as a writing assignment is a relatively late development in composition programs.

Second, the reintroduction of rhetoric into the curriculum would entail the reintroduction of the rhetorical analysis of political, legal, religious, educational, and commercial discourse primarily aimed at persuasion. Some of this analysis is currently carried on in departments of speech communications, but I am suggesting that such analysis should preoccupy all segments of the curriculum. One could argue that the teaching of the analysis of persuasion is even more important than the teaching of the production of persuasion. The mass media powerfully influence us, and we must learn to reflect analytically on the forces transforming our lives. There is probably a good deal of truth in the position maintained by many of the Frankfurt school that, in modern society, we are often totally oblivious to the very powers that mesmerize our lives.[21]

I am not being totally speculative in these suggestions. Students of mine have used rhetoric in high school classrooms, especially with minority students, with some surprising results. Students who are untouched by the importance of writing expository themes or the vitality of reading great literature are often suddenly and vividly impressed with the relevance of religious and commercial persuasion to their lives. Kierkegaard's claim that rhetoric is engaging holds even for high school students in Laredo, Texas, or New Iberia, Louisiana. Minority students see, sometimes more vividly than other students, the massive effects of commercial, racial, and political rhetoric on their lives. Advertisements in grocery stores, which we often interpret as merely informative, strike them as coercive and unfair, for example.

The Renaissance talked about Lady Rhetoric, but the Greeks had a goddess of persuasion called Peitho (literally, "I believe"). Like many of the gods and goddesses, she was presented ambivalently in literature and sculpture. With Eros and Aphrodite, she moved in the ambience of the marriage circle of goddesses, a fact that itself has been given several interpretations. But in some contexts she was also one of the graces, and she consistently exemplified the freedom to make up one's own mind. Tacitus, the Roman historian, remarked that rhetoric was emphasized wherever free political systems existed and ignored in the empire.

I would like to make a rhetorical plea for the return of Peitho to high school and college classrooms. She has been in exile entirely too long.

Notes

[1] The Commission on the Humanities, *The Humanities in American Life* (Berkeley: Univ. of California Press, 1980). This paper was originally delivered as a reaction to this particular section of the report, at the MLA Convention in Houston, Texas, Dec. 1980. Further references to this report will appear in the text.

[2] *Report of the Commission on the Humanities*, sponsored by the American Council of Learned Societies (New York: ACLS, 1964).

[3] Diogenes Laertius, *Lives of the Philosophers*, trans. R. D. Hicks, Loeb Classical Library (London: William Heinemann, Ltd., 1925), II, 70.

[4] Fritz R. Wehrli, "Vom antiken Humanitätsbegriff," *Theoria und Humanitas: Gesammelte Schriften zur antiken Gedankenwelt* (Zurich: Artemis Verlag, 1972), p. 12.

5 Werner Jaeger, *Paideia*, trans. Gilbert Highet (New York: Oxford Univ. Press, 1939), III, 46; Henri I. Marrou, *A History of Education in Antiquity*, trans. George Lamb (London: Sheed & Ward, 1956), pp. 267–68; Bruno Snell, *The Discovery of the Mind: The Greek Origins of European Thought*, trans. T. G. Rosenmeyer (Oxford: Basil Blackwell, 1953), p. 248; Moses Hadas, *Humanism: The Greek Ideal and Its Survival* (New York: Harper, 1960), pp. 61–67, 87.

6 See Wehrli for the references; on the relation of the term *philanthropia* to *humanitas* see Wehrli, pp. 13–14, and Snell, p. 254.

7 Homer, *The Iliad of Homer and the Odyssey*, trans. Samuel Butler, Vol. 4 of Great Books of the Western World, ed. Robert M. Hutchins (Chicago: Encyclopaedia Britannica, 1952), IX.111–16. Wehrli relates this tradition to the concept of *humanitas*, referring to this and other passages in Homer, Hesiod, Protagoras, the tragedians, the historians, and Isocrates, pp. 8, 13–14.

8 See Isocrates, "Antidosis," 253–57, in *Isocrates*, trans. George Norlin (Cambridge: Harvard Univ. Press, 1968), II:
> For in the other powers which we possess, as I have already said on a former occasion, we are in no respect superior to other living creatures; nay, we are inferior to many in swiftness and in strength and in other resources; but, because there has been implanted in us the power to persuade each other and to make clear to each other whatever we desire, not only have we escaped the life of wild beasts, but we have come together and founded cities and made laws and invented arts; *and, generally speaking, there is no institution devised by man which the power of speech has not helped us to establish.* (my italics)

9 Hadas, pp. 8–24; Snell, "On Human versus Divine Knowledge," esp. pp. 144–52.

10 Snell, p. 250. Isocrates, "Panegyricus," 50, in *Isocrates*, Vol. I.

12 Jaeger, III, 79; Hadas, "The Ecumenical Ideal," pp. 61–67, devotes a central section to Isocrates; J. Jüthner, "Isokrates und die Menschenheitsidee," in *Isokrates*, ed. Friedrich Seck (Darmstadt: Wissenschaftliche Buchgesellschaft, 1976), pp. 122–24.

13 René Antoine Gauthier, O.P., and Jean Yves Jolif, O.P., *Aristote: L'Ethique à Nicomaque*, II (Louvain: Publications Universitaires de Louvain, 1959), 467–70. For primary sources, see "Antidosis," 233–34, 271.

14 Jaeger, III, 321–22, n. 126, talking about "Antidosis," 233–34.

15 John Henry Cardinal Newman, "Knowledge Its Own End," *The Idea of a University*, ed. Martin J. Svaglic (New York: Rinehart, 1960), pp. 73–74.

16 Donald Lemen Clark, *Rhetoric in Greco-Roman Education* (New York: Columbia Univ. Press, 1957), pp. 177–211.

17 See Paul de Man, *Allegories of Reading: Figural Language in Rousseau, Nietzsche, Rilke, and Proust* (New Haven, Conn.: Yale Univ. Press, 1979).

18 Søren Kierkegaard, "Concluding Unscientific Postscript," *A Kierkegaard Anthology*, trans. Walter Lowrie, ed. R. Bretall (New York: Random,

1959), pp. 107, 202–03, 210–14, 220–21, 228–30; and *The Point of View of My Work as an Author: A Report to History and Related Writings,* trans. Walter Lowrie, ed. Benjamin Nelson (New York: Harper, 1962), pp. 26, 29, 33.

[19] Henry Oldfather, *The Greek Literary Texts from Greco-Roman Egypt* (Madison: Univ. of Wisconsin Press, 1923), pp. 80–81.

[20] H. L. Pinner, *The World of Books in Classical Antiquity* (Leiden: Sijthoff, 1948), pp. 43–44.

[21] See Herbert Marcuse, *One-Dimensional Man: Studies in the Ideology of Advanced Industrial Society* (Boston: Beacon, 1966).

PART TWO
Historical Rhetoric Reapplied

4

The *Phaedrus* Idyll as Ethical Play: The Platonic Stance

VIRGINIA N. STEINHOFF

Plato's *Phaedrus* stands on a critical tangent to Aristotelian approaches to rhetorical invention: a speculative document and a literary artifact that shapes a dramatic and ironic stance toward the ancient debate on the nature, ends, and scope of the rhetorical arts.[1] Aristotle excludes from the *Rhetoric* the dialectic and all other arts that provide the speaker's thesis, for he sees them as antecedent to the invention of arguments and the use of persuasion.[2] The *Phaedrus*, however, examines the given, that in discourse which will be remembered, and presents the dialectic as a means of seeking fundamental truths through sustained critical conversation that analyzes and finally transcends the terms of an inadequate rhetorical performance.

The critical difference between the Aristotelian and Platonic theses on the relation between dialectic and rhetoric is thus a matter of emphasis and narrative order rather than of definition, for both assert that noble rhetoric is grounded in dialectical procedures. But while Aristotle can set aside dialectical puzzles to proceed with the analysis of the art of persuasion, Plato embeds rhetorical performance and critique in the larger framework of dialectical discourse, which not so much precedes as supersedes rhetoric because of the greater capacity of dialectic for discovering what we ought to examine. The *Phaedrus* adheres more closely to the order and setting of those discoveries than does the *Rhetoric*.

This critical difference in emphasis matches a critical distinction in presentation. Aristotle sets forth a hierarchy of categories by which we can judge the superiority of logical appeals, and then he proceeds to anatomize these appeals and their less noble relatives (appeals to passions and fears) with unequal regard for the hierarchy he proposes. In the *Phaedrus*, however, we see what Richard M.

31

Weaver has called the "dramatistic presentation of a major thesis," that of *form*.[3] Plato's examination of this thesis maintains the sense of hierarchy, of order and proportion, that Aristotle disregards. While Aristotle's theory may be recontextualized piecemeal, Plato's theory is an interlaced pattern of implications. Consequently, the *Phaedrus* has generated no models or schools of rhetorical theory, while Aristotle's *Rhetoric* has proved wonderfully adaptable for later times. Platonic approaches in contemporary theory and teaching may be recognized not so much from their paradigmatic filiations as from their integrity of shape and obliqueness of attack. We may recognize a distinct direction of thought or startling tone, or we may perceive that the rhetorical issues take impulse from some large, transcendent frame of reference that commits the shaper to metaphorical implication and patterns of analogy. We sense someone with a vision, or perhaps a polemical tendency. These approaches are frequently charged with obscurantism and impracticality, with a violation of convention.

In establishing a new frame of reference, a hierarchical critique, a dialectical polemic, or a mythic narrative, people who worry about the ungivenness of the given may appear blind to the virtues and comprehensiveness of the Aristotelian eye for detail and for the conventional and productive style of explication. As they hold up the business of getting on with what can be got on with, they may seem perversely impractical and antirhetorical, or illiberal and cranky. Nevertheless, in times when rhetoric is stripped of all but arrangement and style (by Ramus or behaviorism or, as some would say, by sentence combining), these Platonic critics may rescue the art from shame, clothing its more beautiful body with wings—or power. Insofar as rhetorical history is dialectic, a conversation over time between Aristotelian and Platonic critics, its dialectical critics have worked on the side of the angels, toward syntheses of theory, practice, and character that take untranslatable shapes from their makers. These shapes are more often questions than answers, reminders than *dicta*. Rarely can they be reduced to specific pragmatic applications outside the context of new individual syntheses. This angelic elusiveness may evoke the return of Aristotelian solidity to balance the conversation.

Therefore, this essay does not extract many practicable lessons from Plato for teachers of writing; it only sets out to imply what might prove a congenial ethical inheritance for teachers and writers who worry about givens and about the play of irony in their performances. It does not offer a comprehensive reading of Plato's assertions in the *Phaedrus* about the relations among love, dialectic, rhetoric, and written speech, nor will it demonstrate the rhetorical means that Socrates uses to mount his critique of rhetoric. In his essay "The *Phaedrus* and the Nature of Rhetoric," Richard Weaver accomplishes these aims and much more (pp. 3–26). Nevertheless, this essay presumes some familiarity with Weaver's comprehensive sense of the "ethics" of rhetoric and with the play of that term in his personal synthesis of the rhetorical tradition. Because Weaver's essay does not concern itself specifically with the intramural teaching of discourse, we will consider Socrates as teacher and the consequences of his performance for his student Phaedrus. Perhaps their dialogue—a drama in a distinctly idyllic setting outside the walls of Athens—will take us, as it took Weaver, "some distance from the banks of the Ilissus" and back into today's writing classrooms as well.

As Plato reminds us, Socrates never established a school within walls or confined himself to the society of the city. How tactless, then, to draw him into our four walls, especially since he shows such relish for his "retreat" under the shade of the plane tree by the river:

> Here is the lofty, spreading plane tree and the agnus castus, high clustering with delightful shade. Now that it is in full bloom, the whole place will be wonderfully fragrant; and the stream that flows beneath the plane is delightfully cool to the feet. To judge from the figures and images, this must be a spot sacred to Achelous and the Nymphs. And please note how welcome and sweet the fresh air is, resounding with the summer chirping of the cicada chorus. But the finest thing of all is the grass, thick enough on the gentle slope to rest one's head most comfortably. It turns out, dear Phaedrus, that you're the best of guides for a stranger. (p. 7)

This is the only Socratic dialogue set outside Athens, and, as the description suggests, the setting is a *locus amoenus* of natural and mythological resonance far removed from the city streets. Let us therefore see the *Phaedrus* as a pedagogical idyll, an escape from high seriousness into light irony and fresh scents, accompanied by a comic chorus of talky human beings–turned–crickets, from which pragmatic advice is not to be forced by earnest spirits. The recounting of the events of this dialogue is deliberately colloquial and ironic.

Phaedrus meets Socrates in the morning. They agree to walk outside the city by the Ilissus to hear a speech by Lysias that Phaedrus has been studying because he finds its plea that a boy accept a nonlover before a lover both ingenious and unexpected. Socrates professes enthusiasm for this plan because it will be a vacation from his usual activities. Socrates teases Phaedrus until Phaedrus admits that he has a written transcript of the speech up his sleeve, and so they settle down under the plane tree next to the river to hear Phaedrus perform it. As promised, Lysias' speech argues that a young person should accept the favors of a nonlover in preference to those of a lover for many prudent reasons enumerated by the inexhaustible, if passionless, nonlover.

The speech is tedious and tangled, but Socrates astonishes Phaedrus, who must have delivered it con brio, by praising (faintly) only its terseness and well-polished vocabulary: "[T]he language was clear and precise, turned out in accurately balanced periods" (p. 12). When pressed to explain his statement that he "listened to it merely as a piece of rhetoric," Socrates plays the amateur; he seems somewhere to have heard better orations on the same theme—(Plato, p. 13). Phaedrus presses for examples, and Socrates consents to show what can be done with the theme by forcing himself to recall the ideas that "come, I suppose, from some other source, flowing in through my ears, filling me like a pitcher," although he denies that he intends to "compose a different speech more elaborate than [Lysias'] and surpass him in skill" (pp. 13–14). When he agrees to essay the second speech of the morning, he claims to be embarrassed and delivers the speech with his cloak drawn up over his head:

> I shall speak with my head covered to rush through it as quickly as I can. I'm afraid that if I catch your eye I may be ashamed and falter. (p. 15)

Socrates begins by defining love as madness, as the irrational desire for beauty untempered by reason, an approach that, through Socrates' maneuvering, Phaedrus concedes is a commonplace that Socrates may "take for granted" (p. 7). He does, but as the third speech shows, his concept of love differs greatly from what Phaedrus has anticipated when he allows Socrates to ground even his false speech in this definition. Having established his ground dialectically, if not nobly, Socrates reviews the three baleful effects on the beloved of a lover's madness and folly: first, damage to property and repute; second, the loss of good physical conditioning; and third, the loss of spiritual conditioning. Socrates concludes by describing the state of the beloved's feelings when the lover's passion has cooled and rash promises have failed: "As wolf loves lamb, / so lovers love their lads" (p. 21).

Phaedrus is certainly an enthusiastic audience for speeches. He thinks this effort so good that he encourages Socrates to continue, to balance the censure of the lover with praise of the nonlover.

Socrates demurs rather curtly, refusing to waste words on fairly obvious correspondences. Besides, he had better cross the river and get back to town. Barefoot and without a blackboard, he can easily desert his *locus amoenus* and return to Athens. Perhaps he truly intends to break off his dialogue with Phaedrus at this point, perhaps he means to leave his "little tale . . . to the fate it deserves." But Phaedrus begs him to stay; it's almost noon, he notes, adding: "Let's wait and talk about what's been said" (p. 22).

Socrates turns from tucking up his garments and comments, surprisingly, on Phaedrus' "wonderful and sublime" attitude toward the speeches that Phaedrus has either delivered himself or "in some way forc[ed] others to deliver" (Plato, p. 22). His comment is surprising because Phaedrus has expressed a desire for dialogue—a discussion of what has been said—and not for speeches.

Nevertheless, Socrates, who has just alluded to his fatigue and the lack of inspiration that comes from "these Nymphs to whom you have deliberately exposed me," now prepares to deliver yet another speech inspired by Phaedrus' enthusiasm. Phaedrus can only ask, "But how is this? What discourse?" Socrates then changes tone and direction by acknowledging a larger frame of reference for their discourses on the theme of love. He claims to have heard a voice forbidding him to leave the shade of the plane tree until he has propitiated Eros and "made atonement for an impiety to heaven." His speech against the lover has blasphemed a great god: it was "fatuous, and also concealed something impious" (p. 22).

Thus, Socrates responds ironically to Phaedrus' request for critical discussion with the longest sustained monologue of the day and corrects the irony of his second speech by uncovering his head and uncovering the fullness of his dialectical ground, a concealed etymological pun. (Plato's etymology may be questioned, but not Socrates' playful performance of it.) Socrates begins with an etymological argument based on the ancient unity of *mantic* and *manic* states:

> Our ancestors . . . testify to the fact that in proportion as prophecy is superior in value and perfection to augury, both in name and in fact, so also is madness nobler than sanity: the first proceeds from a god, the other from mere man. (p. 26)

This speech, following the recantation, purposes to honor the divine source of the lover's passion and to put erotic love in the context of the soul's quest for beauty and the truth of Being. Proceeding by definition and division but ruled this time by the mythic narrative of the soul's impulse through time and through lower levels of awareness, the speech distinguishes degrees of success in the great quest, particularizing the special advantages of the philosopher and his beloved.

The most striking and memorable element of the speech is the image of the soul as a charioteer with two ill-matched horses. With this image, Socrates shows us the tensions and divine impulses of love. An understanding of what the soul's form "really is" would require "a divine and very long discourse," but "what it resembles . . . may be expressed more briefly and in human language" (p. 28). Having established the usefulness of resemblance, Socrates elaborates on the fates of lovers who control their "wanton" horses and "free the source of goodness" to varying degrees. He who guides himself and his beloved to "an orderly and philosophical way of life" escapes earth and flesh with "full-grown wings" at the end of life. He who offers only "niggardly and transitory gifts," the signs of a suppressed eroticism, we presume, leaves the beloved to "float for 9000 years around the earth and beneath it—a fool!" (pp. 41–42).

Socrates concludes the speech with a prayer to Love. He hopes that his speech will erase his earlier false discourse and that all remaining errors will be attributed to the lingering influence of Lysias, whom he trusts will turn to philosophy someday himself. Socrates remarks slyly that the poetical elements of the speech (such as the chariot image) should be attributed to his desire to please Phaedrus and that perhaps he was a bit carried away (p. 42).

This speech shifts the day's conversation to a project that Phaedrus had surely not anticipated when he invited Socrates for a stroll. At any rate, he feels no need to dine; his appetite for conversation is, if anything, intensified by the more than ingenious exchange of roles and theses. The conversation that follows Socrates' second speech reveals more fully the dialogue's many themes than the limited topics of virtue and eloquence would have permitted. Hereafter, Phaedrus and Socrates discuss the complexities of love and discourse, the dialectic and rhetoric, the relative worth of speech and writing, and the role of the ethical speaker/teacher. Phaedrus begins with an "absurd" critique of Lysias as a mere speech writer (based on secondary opinions), but Socrates counters this approach with a dialectical refutation that sets the scene for the afternoon (p. 42).

In the course of their discussion, Phaedrus abandons his initial theory of rhetoric as the art of arrangement tied to the opinions of the audience. He tempers his former enthusiasm for well-polished speeches with some exercises in analysis, through which the flaws of Lysias' speech are thoroughly exposed. Phaedrus comes to a new understanding: no orator can succeed in the difficult art of right rhetoric without being a philosopher, that is, a seeker of true Being as well as a student of opinions. The following (rather unequal) catechism on a serious science of rhetoric suggests the skepticism we inherit from Plato about rhetorical handbooks that presume scientific authority. Socrates begins the excerpt:

> [T]o be sure, no scientific inquirer should have any resemblance to the blind or the deaf. Evidently, a man who addresses words to another in a scientific manner will accurately describe the nature of the object to which the student is going to apply the speeches. And this, I suppose, will be the soul.
>
> *Phaedr.* Of course.
>
> *Socr.* Then all his effort will be concentrated on this, for it is in the soul that he is endeavoring to implant conviction. Isn't that true?
>
> *Phaedr.* Yes.
>
> *Socr.* So it is plain that Thrasymachus or anyone else who seriously offers a science of rhetoric must first with all possible accuracy describe the soul and make us perceive whether its nature is single and uniform or, like the body, complex; for to do this, we declare, is to describe the nature of anything.
>
> *Phaedr.* Unquestionably.
>
> *Socr.* And in the second place he will state what object it is its nature to act upon, and what it does to this object; or what affect it is its nature to experience and under the influence of what agent.
>
> *Phaedr.* Of course.
>
> *Socr.* And in the third place, when he has arranged in an ordered series the kinds of discourse and the types of soul together with their affections, he will proceed to give an account of causation that is complete for the entire series, linking each affection to its corresponding cause. That will show why, when a soul is of one sort and is acted upon by a certain sort of speech, it is necessarily moved to persuasion; and why, in another case, persuasion necessarily fails.
>
> *Phaedr.* That, I think, would be absolutely splendid.
>
> *Socr.* I cannot assert too strongly, my friend, that if any subject, and particularly the one we are concerned with, is explained or described in any other way, it will never lend itself to scientific statement, whether oral or written. Our contemporaries—you've heard of them—who write handbooks

on rhetoric are crafty fellows who keep to themselves this matter of soul, though they know it perfectly well. So until they compose their works and speeches by this method let us refuse to believe their statement that they write "scientifically." (p. 63)

Socrates here adduces three extremely challenging criteria for any rhetorical paradigm, Aristotelian or contemporary. Later, Socrates admits that "the path is long and circuitous." He concedes that the goal, although unattainable, does redeem the effort expended to reach it: "Well, even an attempt to reach the good is probably good for one—I mean whatever experience an attempt may bring (p. 63).

After this concession to the validity of rhetorical studies and the honor of rhetorician students, Socrates leads Phaedrus to ask him to recount "what I've heard from our ancestors" about the "propriety and impropriety of writing." Thus invited, Socrates tells the mythical anecdote of Theuth, the inventor of writing, and of Thamus, its judge. This apparently casual segue from rhetorical science to literary art returns the dialectic to a consideration of the effects of unmediated discourse, which allows souls to "rely on what is written, calling things to mind no longer from within themselves by their own unaided powers, but under the stimulus of external marks that are alien to themselves" (p. 68). Socrates associates Phaedrus with the other "pupils" who look at writing as at pictures, which "maintain a solemn silence" when questioned and have "no notion of whom to address or whom to avoid" (p. 70).

The silent and solemn written discourse implies an alternative mode and style, a "legitimate brother of our bastard":

A discourse which is inscribed with genuine knowledge in the soul of the learner; a discourse that can defend itself and knows to whom it should speak and before whom to remain silent. (p. 70)

This discourse, neither silent nor solemn, is congenial soil for new discourse, just as the natural setting by the Ilissus has proved congenial to the play and sowing of fresh words. Socrates abandons the picture analogy to describe a farmer-teacher who

when he does use writing ... will be sowing the forcing-areas of written-expression, as it were, for the mere fun of it, even though he may be packing away a treasury of reminders against an old age of forgetfulness, if he ever reaches it—and not only for his own use, but for any other's whose

goal is the same as his. It will delight him to watch the delicate, forced bloom of his plants; and while others are engaged in various other amusements, refreshing themselves
with banquets and the like, he will presumably prefer to
spend the time he devotes to play in such activity as I have
suggested. (p. 71)

Thus, the dialogue has returned to the metaphors of its beginning and now comments on the form and tone of the whole before
the time for play is over. Pedagogical idylls must come to an end.

As they turn back to Athens at the end of the afternoon, Socrates asks Phaedrus to take a message to Lysias that urges Lysias
to be more than a mere speech writer or poet or drafter of laws, to
take up more serious pursuits that would cause him to be called a
lover of wisdom, a philosopher. Phaedrus asks Socrates to carry another message to his own beloved friend, Isocrates, who already has
a "tincture of philosophy" in his thought (p. 74).

Socrates does not, as it were, take Phaedrus into his own
garden or raid Lysias' "classroom" by keeping a new pupil enchant-
ed forever by play on the riverbank, lulled by the songs of crickets.
Instead of alienating Phaedrus' affections and allegiance, he suggests a new community for the future, a community without walls,
spatial or temporal, except for those inevitable differences between
the friends "within me" and the friends without, the complexity of
each soul and the subtleties of the movement of souls in time. While
his hopes for Isocrates are greater than his fears about Lysias' use
of inferior powers, he nevertheless releases Phaedrus to his beloved.

Socrates pauses to pray to the gods of the place for wisdom
and temperance, a prayer that pleases Phaedrus, too, "for friends
hold everything in common" (p. 75). And so they depart.

To find pragmatic applications in this case study in prayerful
teaching for contemporary writing teachers requires more than in-
terpretive exegesis and more than a translation of the Athenian
ethos, the Platonic ethic, and the Socratic ethical appeal. As I assert-
ed earlier, the Platonic stance toward rhetorical arts and instruction
is synthetic and artful, shaped from unexpected material into new
forms that are, at best, suggestions of things not seen. The Socratic
role requires, in addition, a kind of playfulness and suspension of
goal-directed behavior that is unlikely to sit well with responsible institutions of higher learning or teachers anxious about productivity
in the classroom, specifically about written products—papers, essays, themes, theses, scholarly articles, and so on. If we wrenched
dicta for instruction from Socrates' performance on the banks of the

Ilissus, we might come up with something like the following recipe for professional suicide:

(1) Don't profess what you know (or remember) too readily. Make the students ask for it, and then surprise them by appearing not to comply.

(2) Profess less knowledge and sophistication than your students. Go barefoot whenever possible and try to get them to make fun of you. Enjoy all this.

(3) Use a lot of questionable pseudo-historical anecdotes to assert important points. When pressed for interpretation, assume a pious and literal persona.

(4) Bewilder your students with metaphors and images so that you can avoid lengthy explications of crucial propositions, but be sure to tune these complicated and unstable discourses to the complicated and unstable souls of your students. One student at a time is enough.

(5) Once you have achieved a rapport with a student, keep the student with you until the play of ideas and language satisfies you with its formal and ideological consonances and then break off instruction.

(6) Make fun of yourself, and go ahead, be ironic: students should go away with so many questions about you, as well as about your discourse, that you risk scandal and oblivion in the long run. But know you were right to anticipate this and incorporate it into your teaching. Some students will long remember you.

(7) Put nothing in writing, but talk so well that one of your students is driven to the forcing-area, impelled to memorialize or utilize you for purposes beyond your own prophetic vision. And certainly don't write textbooks.

In his introduction to the 1956 edition of the *Phaedrus*, translated by himself and W. G. Rabinowitz, W. C. Helmbold discusses the larger ironies of Plato's choice of light irony as a unifying tone for the whole dialogue, which "attack[s] literature in one of the most self-conscious pieces of writing that the ancient world produced." He wonders, "Is it fanciful to imagine Plato providing a humorous justification for Socrates' failure to leave anything in writing? (p. xv). By the same token, is it fanciful to imagine Plato's providing a humorous justification for and qualification of his own written composition, which allows us to apply his ironies to ourselves; should we be so bold as to risk reproach in order to avoid sterility? Near the end of the dialogue, Socrates sketches a hierarchy of honor to explain what circumstances for writing may or may not "properly involve reproach" (pp. 72–73). After characterizing those who write expedient politic documents in the service of the mob as disgraceful, Socrates continues:

> On the other hand, there is the man who thinks that the written word on any subject necessarily contains much that is playful, and that no work, whether in verse or prose, has even been written or recited that is worthy of serious attention—and this applies to the recitations of rhapsodes also, delivered for the sake of mere persuasion, which give no opportunity for questioning or exposition—the truth is that the best of these works merely serves to remind us of what we know already. However, complete lucidity and serious importance, he will think, belong only to those lessons in justice and beauty and goodness which are delivered for the sake of true instruction and are, in fact, inscribed in the soul; such discourses as these should be counted as his own legitimate children, a name to be applied first to those that take their source within himself, and secondarily to any of their offspring or brothers that may have worthily been implanted within the souls of others. To other kinds of discourse he will pay no attention. Such a man as this, Phaedrus, is probably the sort of man that you and I might do well to pray we might become. (p. 73)

The language is sufficiently ambiguous to allow for some written discourses to be "inscribed in the soul" as well as with ink on paper, but it hammers persistently at the theme of the possible-impossible philosopher's man, who goes not by steps (not even in that reification, "the writing process") but by the generation of discourse in souls who find lucid those dialogues that concern the ethical and aesthetic ideals most of us find so difficult to articulate, let alone profess.

In a most general sense, then, the Platonic inheritance must be transcended through individual and complex souls, ethical performers who shape their instruction with character and language. Like Socrates, these teachers have style, which is at once unspecifiable and inimitable, yet significant and illimitable. The Platonic inheritance is necessarily committed and personal and is often transmitted orally or through fugitive materials transcribed only as aids to memory and revision. Occasionally, statements will issue from unexpected directions where this personal yet social worrying has been enjoyed. These statements can be recognized by their synthetic approach and intransigent style. For example, Richard Ohmann examines the ideological implications of using clarity and orderliness as the ultimate terms for contemporary school writing in *English in America: A Radical View of the Profession.*[4] In *The Plural I*, William E. Coles, Jr. shows

> how one instructional plan was employed at one college in one recent semester by one instructor in his teaching of writing. In showing the process of that teaching, the book dramatically represents the enactment of teaching techniques. In showing that enactment, it implies—though it never states overtly—a theory of discourse that might be the basis of a unifying rhetoric.[5]

Such enactments, statements, and occasional polemics issue from people I would call contemporary Platonic rhetorical theorists. Although often difficult to read, because they assume a context that cannot always be explicated as well as it can be dramatized, these materials ought to be recognized and savored, both as correctives to Aristotelian analysis when it appears to mount scientific claims that shift the responsibility for writing from the writer to a methodology without "soul" and as respite from the labor of teaching writing in a time when playfulness and artfulness are not perceived as serious pedagogical duties.

As for one's own composition teaching, is it not always in some sense a dialectical enactment, whether acknowledged as such or not? The casual and unpremeditated expressions of style that teachers and students notice and sometimes discuss follow a narrative order from the first class meeting to the last comment and question. And beyond the composition classroom, teachers and students enact the great drama of social history in the characters they teach each other to perform, for with language we have all things in common, whatever the current trends or exigencies of the profession of rhetorical art.

Instead of concluding with specific recommendations for reading or practice, which would offer the kind of surface lucidity that Socrates avoids because to him it obscures the play of language, ethos, and dramatic moment, this essay will borrow a device from Ann Berthoff, who provides what we may call a Platonic critique of Janice Lauer's article and bibliography, "Heuristics and Composition," with a sampling of "some observations and comments which I have found to have heuristic value."[6] Lauer and Berthoff debate the problem of invention in an exchange of views that enacts, once again, the distinctly tangential stances of the Aristotelian and the

Platonic *ethos*. Lauer, it should be noted, replies to Berthoff's critique with tact and considerable synthesis, although she is bewildered by Berthoff's failure to see that their views on the breadth of context essential for a truly powerful new theory of invention are compatible. This failure strikes me as just the sort of fruitful misapprehension of the "other stance" that makes contemporary dialogue on rhetorical issues as lively and productive as it is. Both Lauer's extensive bibliography and Berthoff's congerie of voices seem valuable reminders of what we do not know; but on the Platonic tangent, we choose the more playful and ironic approach of quotation out of context to suggest the adumbrations of future offspring that flicker on the walls of our present dark station.

> The social context of English composition courses cannot be defined in either political or psychological terms unless it is understood in philosophical terms and that means asking where it is indeed that our students are, not assuming that they are "nonverbal," as was the custom a few years ago, or that they are "linguistic adults," meaning not "language animals" but well-programmed encoders.[7]
>
> —ANN E. BERTHOFF

> How should I know what I can *mean* when I don't even know . . .
> How should I know what I *can* mean unless I try?
> How should I know what *I* can mean when I don't know what . . .
> How should I know *what* I can mean—quite a lot so far!
> How should I *know* what I can mean when I feel I must guess?
> How should *I* know what I can mean—ask the experts!
> How *should* I know what I can mean if not this way?
> *How* should I know what I can mean? You shall teach me.[8]
>
> —MARTIN JOOS

> Next to the problem of what accounts for the fact that a man moves at all is the problem of the direction his movement will take.[9]
>
> —GEORGE A. KELLY

> The learner, like the discoverer, must believe before he can know. But while the problem-solver's foreknowledge expresses confidence in himself, the intimations followed by the learner are based predominantly on his confidence in others; and this is an acceptance of authority.

Such granting of one's personal allegiance is—like an act of heuristic conjecture—a passionate pouring of oneself into untried forms of existence.[10]

—MICHAEL POLANYI

We classify at our peril. Experiments have shown that even the lightest touch of the classifier's hand is likely to induce us to see members of a class as more alike than they actually are, and items from different classes as less alike than they actually are. And when our business is to do more than merely look, these errors may develop, in the course of our dealings, into something quite substantial. Yet, in the present state of our knowledge about the way we perceive differences and similarities, the process of classifying seems an essential stage on the way to understanding our environment, or indeed responding to it even in more practical ways: if we see somebody throw something at us we may well spend the split second wondering what category of missile it is—as well as ducking!

—JAMES BRITTON, TONY BURGESS, NANCY MARTIN,
ALEX MCLEOD, HAROLD ROSEN

. . . the student of rhetoric must realize that in the contemporary world he is confronted not only by evil practitioners, but also, and probably to an unprecedented degree, by men who are conditioned by the evil created by others. The machinery of propagation and inculcation is today so immense that no one avoids entirely the assimilation and use of some terms which have a downward tendency. It is especially easy to pick up a tone without realizing its trend. Perhaps the best that any of us can do is to hold a dialectic with himself to see what the wider circumference of his terms of persuasion are. This process will not only improve the consistency of one's thinking but it will also, if the foregoing analysis is sound, prevent his becoming a creature of evil public forces and a victim of his own thoughtless rhetoric.[12]

—RICHARD M. WEAVER

The frame then, what the entire activity of writing is to be about and for, in the name of *what* students are going to be invited to work at becoming "better communicators," or "more effective" as writers, or "correct" or "proficient"— this is everything, and for everybody involved.[13]

—WILLIAM E. COLES, JR.

Notes

1 Plato, *Phaedrus*, trans. with introd. by W. C. Helmbold and W. G. Rabinowitz (Indianapolis: Bobbs-Merrill, 1956); hereafter cited parenthetically in the text.

2 Aristotle, *The Rhetoric of Aristotle*, trans. Lane Cooper (Englewood Cliffs, N.J.: Prentice-Hall, 1960), pp. 7–8.

3 Richard M. Weaver, "The *Phaedrus* and the Nature of Rhetoric," in *The Ethics of Rhetoric* (South Bend, Ind.: Gateway-Regnery, 1953), p. 5.

4 Richard Ohmann, *English in America: A Radical View of the Profession* (New York: Oxford Univ. Press, 1976), esp. "Freshman Composition and Administered Thought," pp. 133–71.

5 William E. Coles, Jr., *The Plural I: The Teaching of Writing* (New York: Holt, 1978), p. vii.

6 The four articles are Janice Lauer, "Heuristics and Composition," and "Response to Ann Berthoff: 'The Problem of Problem Solving' "; Ann E. Berthoff, "The Problem of Problem Solving," and "Response to Janice Lauer: 'Counterstatement.' " All are collected in *Contemporary Rhetoric: A Conceptual Background with Readings*, ed. W. Ross Winterowd (New York: Harcourt, 1975), pp. 79–103. The exchange was originally published by the National Council of Teachers of English journal, *College Composition and Communication*, between 1970 and 1972.

7 Berthoff, "The Problem of Problem Solving," in *Contemporary Rhetoric*, p. 96.

8 Martin Joos, *The Five Clocks*, in *Essays on Rhetoric*, ed. Dudley Bailey (New York: Oxford Univ. Press, 1965), p. 307.

9 George A. Kelly, *A Theory of Personality: The Psychology of Personal Constructs* (New York: Norton, 1963), pp. 37–38.

10 Michael Polanyi, *Personal Knowledge: Towards a Post-Critical Philosophy*, corrected ed. (Chicago: Univ. of Chicago Press, 1962), p. 208.

11 *The Development of Writing Abilities 11–18*, A Report from the Schools Council Project on Written Language of 11–18 Year Olds (London: Macmillan Educational, 1975), p. 1.

12 Weaver, "Ultimate Terms in Contemporary Rhetoric," in *The Ethics of Rhetoric*, p. 232.

13 "Teaching Writing, Teaching Literature: The Plague on Both Houses," *Freshman English News*, 9 (Winter 1981), 16.

5

Classical Practice and Contemporary Basics

SUSAN MILLER

I remember attending a workshop at the 1974 NCTE meeting in New Orleans. The crisp teacher who led the session asked us, as you would a class, "What's the first thing you teach when you teach children math?" ADDITION! "And the second?" SUBTRACTION! "The third?" MULTIPLICATION! (We were getting a little bored. But teachers tend to be patient, so we went on to chorus division, geometry, and algebra.)

"Fine," she said. "Now. What's the first thing you teach when you teach writing?"

The room went off like slow popcorn. I'm sure some fairly strong pockets said, "Reading!," "Sentences!," "Grammar!," and "Letters!" I heard a few single voices suggest thesis sentences, spelling, and diagramming. And I'm fairly certain that I was not alone in my almost mute and mindless stammer. All the English teachers in the room were certain about the proper sequence of mathematics instruction, but no two agreed on, and most had not before considered, the same progression in English.

You may not share this confusion. You may see what you teach as a rational sequence of instruction that proceeds step by logical step and produces the advanced literacy we value. But others, at least the faculty I have worked with in Ohio and Wisconsin, find planning the sequence of a curriculum—deciding what to put first, in what course to teach what, what to evaluate at each stage of a student's progress, and especially how to begin and rationally complete writing instruction—their most difficult problem.

I would not want to limit my view of this dilemma to K–12 instruction. This problem accounts for the current war cry of college faculty: they should have had that in high school! With some exceptions, often caused by irrefutable evidence that the students in a freshman class sometimes spell their own names differently from one paper to another, colleges respond to today's reading and writing problems with no program they could call "high school work," or, what is often worse, with a program they treat *only* as ancillary "high school work." Whichever dirt road they take, colleges keep emphasizing that something comes before the highway of college work that the colleges don't know much about. Once "college work" is reached (and few colleges have any clear idea what constitutes that level of ability), the sequence of English instruction exhibits no more rigor than the division of courses into three stages: freshman, introductory, and the rest. Where remedial work is done, no one is quite sure what it should remedy or how to tell when an adult student has in fact been cured. Remedial instruction at Berkeley has little to do with the same "remedial" instruction at the City University of New York. One suspects that no recognized level of advanced literacy now identifies the college-educated person.

When things get as bad as they now are—when teachers at all levels spend as much time as they do explaining and defending the causes of the generally mediocre uses of language that disappoint students' parents and terrify prospective employers, when CBS takes three hours of prime time to elucidate the failure of American education, and when the interaction between high school and college instruction is characterized by stances little more respectable than those of two children with their tongues out—it is time for reconsideration.

In the face of the large advertisements in *Time* that mistake "their" for "there," some still claim that the current level of literacy in our country is in fact no worse than it once was: good students are as good as they ever were. The demography of the school population and especially the college population, however, is now radically enlarged. We can't expect fluency in either reading or writing from the masses who merely pass through twelve years of school and four years of college. Even minimal literacy in so comprehensive a segment of the population is too much to ask. In sum, "most of these students weren't in college before" and "they don't belong here."

This argument appears to have prevailed, for even after ten years of the back-to-basics movement students achieve the same low scores on SAT, ACT, and NAEP examinations. Most responses to the proclaimed literacy crisis in both schools and universities resulted either in more instruction of the kind that contributed to that crisis or in research aimed largely at describing disadvantaged students' mistakes and problems. Few seem to have taken seriously the question that the demographic argument so sharply raises: why wouldn't a broad spectrum of students benefit from the same instruction that worked to educate those who were in school in the past?

A reconsideration, then, might emphasize the substance of basic education as it was defined for hundreds of years in the Western world. The education of the Greek, Roman, medieval, and Renaissance schoolboy (and almost all were boys), and especially the education in reading and composing that through the nineteenth century made those who completed school the models for our view of advanced literacy, seems to me worth considering in view of our current retreat to the basics.

I'm thinking of course of the education prescribed in Cicero's *Education of an Orator* and Quintilian's *Institutes,* a system that was not much different from education in Hellenistic Greece. This program was not only homogenously used in both Greece and Rome but, after Rome was conquered, was also maintained in provincial schools like the North African one that trained Augustine. The sixteenth-century humanists reinstituted organized classical education after the discovery of the complete texts of Cicero's *De Oratore* in 1414 and Quintilian's *Institutio* in 1419.

Then, as now, there were three stages of education. Primary school, which students entered at seven, was taught by the *literator*—the teacher of letters, who was responsible for literacy. Here the students memorized and practiced writing the alphabet and read maxims and proverbs, which they also memorized. At this level, they learned mathematics through fractions and weights and measures. As far as we know, education in primary literacy moved from parts to wholes: students learned letters, syllables, words, and finally sentences.

The next school, grammar school, was taught by a *grammaticus.* At each level, the teachers were specialists; Quintilian made a point of complaining that the *grammaticus* was no *rhetor* and should not extend his teaching of literature into more advanced rhetorical training. At grammar school, however, students learned much more than grammar. From the age of entry at about twelve until advanced rhetorical training at fifteen, students learned not only how to parse sentences correctly, to use new vocabulary, and to speak with the correct accent and pronunciation needed to make effective speeches but also the important literary texts. I say the important texts because to assume that grammar schools taught literature in the sense that we think of teaching literature at any level today is mistaken. Indeed, the students read Homer, Hesiod, Sappho, and the tragedians, but they carefully applied the Roman judicial rhetoric's doctrine of *status* to each work. The questions

"Did something happen?," "What was it?," and "What value did it have?" were transformed in the grammar schools' teaching of literature into a four-part treatment of each text. First the young scholars reconstructed the texts of the works to be read from often fragmented, faulty manuscripts. Then they read the texts, memorizing them and presenting expressive readings to practice public delivery and correct pronunciation. In the third stage, called exegesis or exposition, the students dealt with what the texts meant. They parsed sentences grammatically, defined and learned vocabulary words, studied allusions to geographical, historical, or literary matters, and explained the content of each work. In the fourth and final stage, the class drew moral lessons from the texts. Although this stage was called "criticism," it was never the thematic, generic, or formal analysis of literature we know; rather, it was a demonstration of the moral and ethical use of the work.

Quintilian drew a strict line between this grammar school education, comparable until this century to the first and second forms of preuniversity work, and the work of higher education, which was training in rhetoric. The *grammaticus* was to teach correct speech and proper grammar as well as the texts of the poets. But his work was not to overlap with the work of the *rhetor*, who taught the invention and arrangement of compositions that effectively advised, praised, or decided legal business in the public realm. Although Quintilian's complaint went unheard and grammar schools taught rhetorical exercises, the rhetorician's preserve—turning out citizens educated to participate persuasively in their communities—was clearly defined.

This rhetorical education in advanced schools and universities deserves some attention, for rhetoric was the primary concern of higher education in the Western world until relatively recently. Literary study continued, as did some mathematical and historical study in preparation for accomplished eloquence. Grammar school writing exercises—summarizing stories, paraphrasing, writing narratives, and systematically developing fables, aphorisms, and confirmations or confutations—were more complicated in advanced schools. Students in colleges practiced eulogies and censures, wrote character sketches and descriptions, and argued both sides of theses: whether a man should marry, whether day or night is more beautiful (a topic that Milton also treated), whether it is ethical to poison your enemies in war. Although the Platonic method of debate became dominant in the universities of the Middle Ages during the time when Cicero and Quintilian were lost to scholars, the three arts of language—grammar, rhetoric, and dialectic—were the dominant *trivium* in post-grammar school studies for over a thousand years. The quadrivium of math, music, astronomy, and geometry were also included, and universities later prepared students specifically for sermon writing, law, and medicine. But rhetorical competence was the entire goal of preparatory schools and the core of undergraduate education.

Thus it is interesting to describe what that rhetorical education included and how it fell into the darkness that now surrounds it. If rhetorical education *was* education for fifteen hundred years, what happened to it?

The five domains of rhetoric, for Aristotle and for all the other ancients, were invention, or the discovery of the content of a discourse; arrangement, or deciding in what order to present the content invented; style, or the diction, schemes, tropes, and figures of elegant sentences; memory, or the skill of memorizing what would later be spontaneous and engaging; and delivery, or the control of stance, voice, posture, and audience contact that became the only concern of most nineteenth-century elocutionists. Assignments in composition or debate included each of these five stages, elaborately codified to produce predictably effective results. The question remains, What happened to this discipline? How did rhetoric become the nasty word now usually mentioned only in reference to manipulative politicians and major oil companies?

The divisive history of rhetorical study is a complex tale. It explains, however, the theory and practice in contemporary classrooms now housing that broad spectrum of the population who have so much educational opportunity but so little education. In period after period, century after century, another of the rhetorical domains that originally unified intention, thought, and discourse found a new, specialized disciplinary home. Once Cicero and Quintilian were lost to the Middle Ages, dialectic reigned as the method of undergraduate education. Students argued cases all day with one teacher, with four, and finally with a series of opponents as they moved from the B.A. through the M.A. examinations. Rhetoric was a professional tool used in composing sermons and letters. The discovery of the complete texts of Cicero and Quintilian reintroduced their educational systems, which Italian humanists like Vico argued for in opposition to the results of Cartesan rationalism. It takes little philosophical training to recognize, however, that rhetorical humanism, the view that unites language, thought, and action in the person, lost out to self-reflexive rationalism, the separation of subject from object. The contextuality of rhetoric could not hold sway against objective, scientific, and ultimately positivistic philosophies.

Beginning in the late sixteenth century, Peter Ramus and his student Omer Talon argued influentially that invention and arrangement, the domains of rhetoric in which students learn systematic thinking and the appropriateness of their statements to various audiences, were separate from other rhetorical matters, whose aim they saw as primarily stylistic. Late sixteenth-century books, like the *Arts of Logic and Rhetoric* and *The Two Books of Ramean Logic*, signal in their titles this separation of thinking from rhetoric. Ever since this time we have conceived of thinking as a private act rather than an intentional and public one. The separation of what to say from how to say it was not accomplished before the disciplinary separation of logic from rhetoric, for thought was originally seen as a stage in preparing to address that thought to an audience.

In John Williams' novel, *Augustus*, the contrast between ancient and modern views of rhetoric is vividly portrayed. Augustus' daughter Julia suggests how far we have moved from the original view of thought and expression by beginning her diary, written in exile, by saying that she knows that to embark on the diary is against the rules of her teachers, who would never approve of or understand writing thoughts no one else would ever see.

Clearly the idea that thinking is separate from, much less different from, what we say or write is, as the Renaissance literary and political emphases on deceit and duplicity may reflect, a distinctly postclassical notion. Its consequences guide those who now think it worthwhile to teach writing primarily as a series of stylistic and formal constraints on the prose of advanced students who "already have too much to say." Similarly, those inside and outside departments of English who think that teaching good writing means teaching spelling, grammar, and punctuation also express the postclassical view of the separation of language from thought. Both groups are Ramists unawares; they believe that logic and rhetoric, like invention and style, must belong to separate disciplines, and they teach the one sometimes in ignorance of the corpus of the other.

Only a few years after the influence of Ramus took invention and arrangement away from rhetoric and placed them in philosophy, a similar division of the domains of rhetoric was encouraged by Francis Bacon and others looking for a scientific language to reflect scientific, or empirically verifiable, objectivity. Reason and imagination were separate for Bacon, as were matter (*res*) and words (*verba*). Debates on the relation of matter to words or style to content had been impossible until scholars separated the study of rhetoric into separate disciplines. By the eighteenth and nineteenth centuries, the critics of rhetoric claimed that it was only concerned with ornamental style, with style to the confounding of meaning. Sensitive rhetoricians, having long given up the study of memory, turned to the fifth and only other domain, that of delivery. Thus the elocutionary movement was almost all that remained of specifically rhetorical study by the end of the nineteenth century. Forensics, the art of gesture, became the ghost of classical rhetoric.

The disruption of the study of rhetoric I have recounted did not, of course, cause complete forgetfulness of rhetorical matters at once, in swift blows. Even today, Ohio State University's Department of English is housed in a building commemorating the Francis Denney Department of Rhetoric and Literature. Final blows to the study and teaching of rhetoric have occurred in a chronology we and our grandparents could have watched. It was not until 1850 that Oxford University appointed a professor of literature, an appointment that came after much debate because, it was argued, every educated man had of course read literature as a boy—he need not, certainly, spend time in higher education *studying* literature. The first departments of speech, the new home of disciplinary rhetoric, were founded in 1913; in the early 1920s, one of the few places in America where Aristotle's *Rhetoric* was taught was Cornell University's Department of Speech. Logic had long since been relegated to departments of philosophy; philology and historical linguistics became the provinces of new departments of linguistics. All that we gained from this inevitable response to new knowledge in new disciplines and departments does not replace what we concurrently lost. Graduate departments of literature, where systematic historical, generic, and formal criticism and creative writing are the only appropriate studies, only partially inform teachers of advanced literacy about the historical discipline devoted to discourse. The responsibility for teaching composition remained in departments of English after the rhetoric, logic, and grammar that should inform such instruction went separate ways.

It is therefore no wonder that, in the NCTE workshop in 1976, we could not decide on the first steps in the teaching of writing. It is no wonder that the public and an unfortunately large percentage of our colleagues at all levels think that teaching composition means only teaching handwriting or proofreading. It is no wonder that we marvel at the pastoral age that produced queens who wrote as Elizabeth I wrote or statesmen who spoke with the eloquence of Disraeli. We now have, by and large, public figures who either hire ghostwriters or express themselves with the conviction and eloquence of Eisenhower.

The ancients taught all voting citizens, who, without lawyers or federal forms to complete, had to argue for the restoration of their property in open court. Both new democracy and a new technology—writing—made the individual responsible for mastering rhetorical habits we now so sorely miss, from "thinking on your feet" to "good delivery." Citizens in Greece also had to be critical thinkers, ready for service on juries that numbered five hundred or as members of the executive council, elected monthly.

We, however, generally teach a "rhetoric of textbooks," the amalgam of associational psychology, analytical stylistics, and belles lettres that new rhetoricians in the eighteenth and nineteenth centuries offered in opposition to the elocutionary movement. The lectures of Blair, Campbell, and Whately and the pedagogy of Alexander Bain preserved the diminished discipline of rhetoric through many editions of school texts, where a static mixture of classical and psychological rhetoric rather than an organic, growing tradition of scholarship may be found. In these textbooks and writing assignments, we express, however unintentionally, essentially Romantic ideas about the impossibility of fostering imagination or nurturing creative intentionality. We teach "patterns of organization" for "material" somehow already discovered rather than the original inventive topoi that find and recall content pertinent to a writer's purpose. For example, instead of suggesting that students may find something to say by comparing one thing to another, we teach them how to organize the details of comparisons they have derived from prior observations and good luck. Thus, what developmental system there is now in teaching advanced literacy usually depends on a sequence of Bain's modes of discourse, within which various patterns of organization are more or less appropriate. Most assignments made to developing writers move from narration to description to exposition to persuasion and through forms of texts rather than through intentions and purposes.

Such a system relies on analyses of written texts and particularly suits teachers trained in ⸱e New Criticism, who are comfortable connecting literary descriptⅰⁿ and narration to the teaching of composition. It encourages paradigmatic studies of written discourse. It progresses from two-dimensional patterns that account for space and time in description and narration to three-dimensional patterns of analysis and qualification in exposition and persuasion. But unlike the classical assignments to write aphorisms, fables, eulogies, censures, character sketches, exhortations, or arguments for or against theses, assignments to write modes of discourse or patterns of organization have no purpose. We cannot find examples of descriptive, narrative, expository, or persuasive writing that are purely one mode or another. The readers that we use in college composition classes make noble attempts to classify their selections this way but never, to my knowledge, succeed. Thus students never read purely descriptive or, for that matter, purely comparison-contrast writing. They are hardly inspired to write it.

Nor do such assignments, however artificial they may be for the sake of practice, produce the spirit and sense of intention that meaningful writing requires. Such assignments do not call for the union of abilities—thinking, arranging, choosing style, and presenting material to a specific audience—that classical exercises in composition required. Telling a student only to "write a comparison-contrast paper" is comparable to telling a cook to go to the kitchen and make up the rest of a recipe that says "fold in the stiffly beaten whites of four eggs."

The pickle—perhaps the soufflé—we are in is easy to explain if we look at the basics historically. For years we have looked for the right way to teach writing, argued for one or another way, agreed that different methods work in different settings, and overlooked the disciplinary content of the teaching of writing. Except for those lonely classes at Cornell, this disciplinary content was a secret well kept from students of English until recently. For a number of reasons, I find appealing both this content and the methods and practice in classical schools. Classical education assumed that everyone in school, all the voting citizens and soldiers of the state, could, with diligence, learn how to think about problems and express convincing solutions. Classical education assumed that students are ready for some parts of this study earlier than they are for others and built gradually on one bit of information after another. Classical education offered not only the discipline of rhetoric but discipline itself; it assumed that hard work, constant practice, application, and honest evaluations of quality were educational, not destructive, methods that led to independent adult thinking and speaking.

At the college level, a composition program based on classical education would be guided by three principles:

1. Each writing assignment would demand a "kind" of writing. That is, each assignment would call for students to write a piece for which they could be shown nonstudent models by writers whose situation, purpose, constraints, and intentions they could identify and identify with.
2. Student writing for writing courses would be perceived as an *instance* of writing rather than as the finished artifact of a failed Author. Instead of attempting (always unsuccessfully) to transcend classroom artificiality by making assignments to write, for example, "for your peers," we would embrace the classroom setting as the normal place to write exercises. The audience would consist of the person who reads and per-

haps writes the kinds of compositions assigned, and who can
judge the student essay as an example of practice. In short,
we would admit that this is school.
3. A writer's purpose rather than a mode of discourse or pattern of organization would determine the sequence of assignments. Writing would be perceived as an intentional act
rather than as a conglomerate of "skills," so a series of tasks
recapitulating the progression of a collegiate writer's purposes would be assigned. Students might move, for example,
through increasingly public kinds of writing; they might
complete research notes or analytical reports on one source
before analyzing it in relation to another.

Applying these principles produces neither wildly divergent nor stul-
tifyingly rigid composition courses, but it does preclude moving from
word to sentence to paragraph or through modes and patterns of organization. It also precludes the exclusive use of the information
found in a basic textbook on writing and encourages the use of textbooks only to codify and supplement the teacher's appropriately bet-
ter-schooled understanding of the processes being fostered. These
principles produce a pragmatic, purposeful model of writing instead
of a grammatical or syntactic view.

The syllabi and specific assignments I know best are those
we use now at the University of Wisconsin, Milwaukee, where "basic
writers" begin by copying and imitating, writing fables and character sketches that allow them to master narration and description for
a purpose, interviewing subjects, reading samples of the kind of writing they are attempting, and judging the effect of their writing
against these samples. Students in later courses write definitions, reports of stylistic analyses, summaries, abstracts, feature articles,
practice essay examinations, editorials, refutations, and documented
research. Such assignments comprehend the modes of discourse, patterns of organization, and stylistic devices the textbooks describe
while supplying implicit audiences, purposes, and examples "in nature." In some of our advanced classes, students study, and apply
the principles of, classical and contemporary rhetoric, analyses of the
composing process, and stylistics.

These developmental assignments and courses allow us to
teach from a conceptual base, as we do when we teach literature.
They also acknowledge that early college writing instruction prepares students for the academy, not for personal or vocational writing, which is offered later when specializations have been chosen.
And they unite the settings in which students read with the demand
to write, forcing us all to take critical analytic reading more serious-

ly than we might in limited discussions of the content of a text from a reader. This approach is not unique to us, of course, but neither is it ordinarily acknowledged to be based on classical practices.

We are now more comfortable about establishing unapologetic standards for successful student writing that is neither precollegiate nor postgraduate. Given the sense that our assignments imitate those that guided classical education, we ride long coattails, reassured that the tasks we perform are appropriate for undergraduates. Without a historical and conceptual basis for teaching, it is difficult to be confident that what is being taught just now is appropriate or necessary to learn before moving on. We had become experimenters in methodology rather than professors—those who tell—of matter that we know everyone can learn because we have ourselves learned it. Quintilian comments that teachers of composition should themselves be skilled in composition, and his reasons are as applicable to us as to his Roman audience: "It frequently happens that the more learned the teacher, the more lucid and intelligible his instruction. For clearness is the first virtue of eloquence, and the less talented a man is the more he will strive to exalt and dilate himself . . . rather than his subject" (*Institutes*, Bk. II. iii.8).

If we do not learn this discipline, if we do not know what those who for centuries could write well did know, we are likely to believe that the basics are spelling, diagramming, punctuation, and perhaps comparison-contrast. It is my quiet but deep conviction that such a shallow notion of basic education in literacy will eventually destroy democracy, for the thinking of citizens is all that democratic states can rely on. Great rhetoric has always flourished in times of social and political upheaval, depressing times like those we now face. The American and French revolutions, the American Civil War, the wars against Germany, and the social revolution in America called forth extraordinary written and spoken discourse. In the face of the problems we share today, I would recommend another such outburst of rhetoric. American teachers must reclaim the development of literacy from relative darkness to make their students the capable thinkers and citizens whose absence, and whose replacement by general muddle, we now feel.

Bibliography

The substance touched on, summarized, and cited in this essay is readily available from:
Bain, Alexander. *English Composition and Rhetoric: A Manual.* 2nd ed. London: Longmans, Green, 1869.

————. *Mental Science: A Compendium of Psychology and the History of Philosophy.* 1868; rpt. New York: Arno, 1973.
Baldwin, T. W. *William Shakespeare's Small Latine and Lesse Greeke.* 2 vols. Urbana: Univ. of Illinois Press, 1944.
Cicero. *De Oratore.* Books I-II. Trans. by E. W. Sutton and H. Rackam. Loeb Classical Library. Cambridge: Harvard Univ. Press, 1948. Book III. Trans. by H. Rackham. Loeb Classical Library. Cambridge: Harvard Univ. Press, 1942.
Clark, Donald Lemen. *John Milton at St. Paul's School: A Study of Ancient Rhetoric in English Renaissance Education.* New York: Columbia Univ. Press, 1948.
————. *Rhetoric in Greco-Roman Education.* New York: Columbia Univ. Press, 1957.
Corbett, Edward P. J. "A Survey of Rhetoric." In *Classical Rhetoric for the Modern Student.* 2nd ed. New York: Oxford Univ. Press, 1971, pp. 594-625.
Golden, James, and E. P. J. Corbett. *The Rhetoric of Blair, Campbell, and Whately.* New York: Holt, 1968.
Murphy, James J. *Rhetoric in the Middle Ages: A History of Rhetorical Theory from Saint Augustine to the Renaissance.* Berkeley: Univ. of California Press, 1974.
Quintilian. *Institutio Oratoria.* Trans. by H. E. Butler. 4 vols. Loeb Classical Library. Cambridge: Harvard Univ. Press, 1920–22.
Williams, John. *Augustus.* Harmondsworth, Eng.: Penguin, 1972.

6

Ciceronian Rhetoric and the Rise of Science: The Plain Style Reconsidered

*S. MICHAEL HALLORAN AND
MERRILL D. WHITBURN*

We increasingly hear the terms "plain language" and "plain English" in the corridors of government, business, and industry. Former President Carter's executive order 12044 mandated that regulations be "as simple and clear as possible," and the Office of Management and Budget is currently striving to carry out his order by promoting plain English in federal agencies. HR 6410, a bill that calls for sweeping revision of the writing done by both the federal government and organizations dealing with the federal government, was recently signed into law. Laws calling for the use of plain language are on the books or under consideration in fully half the states. Banks are simplifying their loan forms, insurance companies their policies, and realtors their contracts. Industries like IBM, Bell Laboratories, United Technologies, Sunstrand Aviation, and General Motors are making major commitments to promote plain language in their publications. English teachers of all varieties—literary critics, technical communicators, and rhetoric and composition specialists—are a bit perplexed to find touted as a wonderful innovation what (at least in part) we have been teaching all our lives.

The public spotlight is shining on plain language for a number of reasons. Edwin Newman and William Safire, among others, are promoting an increased sensitivity to language. Organizations like the Document Design Center, Carnegie-Mellon, and Siegel & Gale are working for improved writing in government and business. Perhaps even the feeble cries of English teachers have had some impact, although our failure, more than our success, has focused national attention on communication. Organizations find themselves unable to convey information clearly to others or to understand the information that others convey to them. Part of the problem is sheer ineptitude, an inability to read and write well, a fact of life that assumes crisis proportions in areas like the nuclear power industry. Part of the problem is insecurity, the fear some professionals like lawyers have that a loss of their obscurities would diminish their profession. Part of the problem is ignorance, a complete unawareness that such factors as patent laws, publication specifications, limitations imposed by word-processing equipment, and a lack of publication coordination in multilocation corporations can have a deleterious impact on the communication process.

Whatever the reasons for the public spotlight on plain language, the moment is critical. Government, business, and industry are now making major decisions about the way communication should be shaped and using these decisions to develop programs for word-processing equipment. For instance, the Naval Air Systems Command has mandated that its publications must pass a Comprehensibility Assurance Test that measures twenty-one comprehensibility criteria, including number of words per sentence, number of polysyllabic words, and proportion of graphics to textual material. Each criterion is assigned a mathematical ideal. The ideal has no more than two paragraphs per heading, no fewer than one figure per heading, and no fewer than one index listing per heading. Corporations hoping to serve the Naval Air Systems Command and organizations like it are developing computer programs to measure a publication against comprehensibility criteria. In some corporations, if a publication fails to attain a certain numerical grade on a comprehensibility assurance test, it is sent back to the writer for revision. We are reminded that just fifteen years ago, Walker Gibson built what he called a "model-T style machine."[1] These more recent machines are, by comparison, sleek and flashy gas guzzlers. Once such mathematical criteria become part of word-processing technology, change is difficult. The standards set for publication in the next few years are likely to affect communication for a long time to come.

Lest we scoff too quickly at simplistic mathematical approaches to communication, we might well glance at recent stylistic research. Although certainly more sophisticated, two stylistic ideals in the literature are nevertheless mathematical: (1) the "mature" style, based on the work of Kellog Hunt, John Mellon, Francis Christensen, and many others, and (2) the "communicatively efficient" or "maximally readable" style, advocated by E. D. Hirsch and growing out of the work of Flesch, Gunning, et al.[2] To our knowledge, no one has yet pointed out that together these two ideals constitute a dilemma, for they move in precisely opposite directions. The most reliable measure of stylistic maturity is T-unit length: the greater the average length of T-units (syntactic elements that could be punctuated as complete sentences), the more mature the passage. An important goal of writing instruction based on the concept of stylistic maturity is to have students writing longer T-units at the end of the term than at the beginning. The most reliable measure of readability (communicative efficiency) is sentence length, but the ratio is inverse; the *shorter* the average sentence, the more readable a passage is. A major goal of writing instruction based on the concept of communicative efficiency is to have students writing shorter sentences (or T-units) at the end of the term.

Let us leave this dilemma unresolved for the moment while we recognize that communicators and researchers, in attempting to make style amenable to mathematical treatment, are taking fundamental steps similar to those taken by Newton and other scientific revolutionaries of the late seventeenth century. Like the scientists of yesteryear, they are attempting to take vague terms and give them a precise meaning as quantitative continua; they are trying to decipher the unfamiliar by resolving it into mathematical terms.[3] The similarity takes on added significance when we note that the terms "plain language" and "plain English" echo both the seventeenth-century term "plain style," which scientists of the time heralded as the writing ideal, and the much older notion of a plain style found in classical rhetorical theory. We believe that recent thinking about plain language is rooted in the same simplistic positivism as seventeenth-century views on the plain style and that this positivistic view of the universe is even less appropriate in our own time than it was in the seventeenth century. We hope to show that the beginnings of a much better model for a plain language movement can be found in classical thought on the plain style, particularly that of Cicero.

Toward the Ideal

In Ciceronian rhetorical theory, the plain style is one of three so-called characters of style; the other two are the middle and the grand styles. They form a hierarchy moving from language that seems relatively close to ordinary speech—the plain style—to the most elevated and extraordinary—the grand style. All three styles use the ornamental devices whose description and cataloging make up so much of later rhetorical theory, but in the plain style the ornamentation is supposed to be less apparent. Elaborate prose rhythm is avoided altogether, and syntax is loose rather than periodic. Only those figures of speech that would not seem radically out of place in everyday discourse are used; metaphor is particularly recommended, since it occurs quite naturally in ordinary speech. But while the plain style should seem close to the artlessness of everyday conversation, achieving the effect in formal discourse is, in Cicero's view, a high and difficult art: "plainness of style seems easy to imitate at first thought, but when attempted nothing is more difficult."[4]

The three characters of style grew out of the notion that propriety is one of the chief virtues of style, an insight that dates back at least to Aristotle. While Book III of his *Rhetoric* places heaviest emphasis on clarity as the most important quality of rhetorical style, it also suggests that different genres of rhetoric call for distinct styles and that language as well as argument must be adapted to the demands of a situation and the expectations of an audience.[5] But by comparison with Cicero's discussion in *De Oratore, De Optimo Genere Oratore*, and especially *Orator*, Aristotle's notion of stylistic adaptation is somewhat crude. In Aristotle's view style is simply a matter of genre; distinguishable styles are appropriate for different speaking situations, whether deliberative, forensic, or ceremonial. Cicero associates the three styles with three effects a speaker must work on the audience: the plain style instructs, the middle style delights, and the grand style moves to belief or action. A well-wrought speech will use all three to orchestrate the audience's response according to the speaker's aim. Plain, middle, and grand styles are levels of embellishment and emotional concentration rather than generically distinct modes of language. Stylistic competence consists in the ability to move from level to level, shaping a curve of audience response from intellectual receptivity, to delight, to conviction and commitment. As treated by Cicero, the three styles suggest something like Kenneth Burke's notion of form as "the creation of an appetite in the mind of the auditor, and the adequate satisfying of that appetite."[6]

We think of Cicero's view of the three styles as symphonic and contrast it with a view that associates distinct styles with distinct genres of discourse.[7] The generic view is simpler and probably more commonly held. We find it in Geoffrey of Vinsauf's belief that "the plain style is more appropriate to comedy" and in John of Garland's belief that Vergil uses the "lowest" of the three styles in the *Bucolics* because it is characteristic of "pastoral men."[8] We find it in the Puritans' view that the plain style is theologically correct for transmitting the word of God.[9] And we find it in the seventeenth-century idea that the plain style is the one appropriate vehicle for the expression of scientific truth. Perhaps Cicero's view that the purpose of the plain style is to instruct provides some justification for associating the plain style with science. But Cicero would have disagreed strenuously with the notion that it is possible to separate instructing from pleasing and persuading except in the abstract. He saw these three rhetorical functions, and hence the three styles, as aspects or phases of the single process of communication by which one human intelligence influences another.

Louis Milic attributes to the classical rhetoricians a theory of style that distinguishes sharply between form and content in discourse.[10] For Cicero at least, the rhetorical dualism of which Milic speaks is certainly an oversimplification and possibly a gross misrepresentation. Cicero's view of the relation between rhetorical form and the content of discourse is somewhat difficult to pin down, but he certainly does not assert a clear and sharp dualism. He in fact criticizes Socrates for making just such a distinction, calling Socrates' teachings "the source from which has sprung the undoubtedly absurd and unprofitable and reprehensible severance between the tongue and the brain, leading to our having one set of professors to teach us to think and another to teach us to speak" (*De Oratore* III.xvi.61). Distinction of style is impossible to achieve without worthy ideas; conversely, ideas remain lifeless without stylistic distinction (*De Oratore* III.vi.24).

Thus plainness does not consist in the absence of all stylistic ornaments. Only the more obviously contrived ornaments are to be avoided. Cicero's liberal use of metaphor and simile to instruct us about the nature of the plain style demonstrates that what classical rhetoricians called ornamentation is appropriate and indeed necessary even in discourse meant to instruct:

> ... although it is not full-blooded, it should nevertheless have some of the sap of life, so that though it lack great strength, it may be, so to speak, in sound health.... Just as some women are said to be handsomer when unadorned ... so this plain style gives pleasure even when unembellished.... All noticeable ornament, pearls as it were, will be excluded; not even curling irons will be used; all cosmetics, artificial white and red, will be rejected; only elegance and neatness will remain.
>
> (*Orator* xxiii.76–79)

Note well the word "noticeable"in the statement that "all noticeable ornament will be excluded." The plain style is simply more subtle in its use of the figures of speech. Cicero recognizes what Aristotle had long before pointed out, that a well-turned metaphor or simile can teach us something by making us see a relation we had not recognized. Figures of speech are *ornaments*, but not in the sense of detachable overlay. Ornamentation is the working out at the surface of discourse a principle of order inherent in the substance.[11]

Cicero's critique of the Socratic dualism is not confined to the question of style and substance in discourse. This more narrow question is for him an aspect of a much larger one: what is the relation between wisdom and action in the realm of human affairs? In Socrates' view, the philosopher must stand apart from practical affairs as a detached "gadfly," pursuing wisdom disinterestedly and in isolation. The philosopher serves the practical needs of the commonwealth through criticism. Cicero took strenuous issue with this view of philosophy and rhetoric as distinct and potentially hostile enterprises. His notion that substance and style in discourse are closely interrelated follows from his conviction that contemplation and action, philosophy and rhetoric, must be interrelated in the same fashion. Philosophy without practical concern is vaporous; practical action without philosophical awareness, irrational. Wisdom and eloquence, philosophy and rhetoric, must be joined. The ultimate purpose of both is to create and sustain a human community.

Throughout antiquity, the dominant tradition of rhetoric had similarly emphasized making a community as the greatest human task and achievement. In a passage that by Cicero's time had become commonplace, Isocrates lauded the power of speech for its role in making human communities:

> ... because there has been implanted in us the power to persuade each other and to make clear to each other whatever we desire, not only have we escaped the life of wild beasts, but we have come together and founded cities and made laws and invented arts; and, generally speaking, there is no institution devised by man which the power of speech has not helped us to establish.[12]

Cicero repeats this passage almost verbatim near the beginning of his earliest theoretical treatise, *De Inventione*. The passage encapsulates a view that characterized classical rhetoric and in fact most of classical culture. In contrast to science, which gathered momentum in the seventeenth century and to which we will turn shortly, it valued human institutions and arts more than knowledge of the physical world.

The Ciceronian plain style, then, could not be measured in abstract quantitative terms. It was a verbal register, the most subtle and quiet one of three, across all of which a person ranged in the effort to move an audience. Its specific function was to instruct people, and its end was to make them a people, a human community with shared goals and values.

Retreat from the Ideal

Developments after Cicero led apologists for the new science in the seventeenth century to call for a revolution in style. Indeed, as Richard Foster Jones writes of these apologists, "We may say without exaggeration that their program called for stylistic reform as loudly as for reformation in philosophy."[13] The same assumptions that led to the advent of scientific method profoundly revolutionized style, and the successes of science ossified that stylistic tradition. Our tradition of the plain style in technical and public discourse is as rooted in the late seventeenth century as the scientific revolution itself is. This tradition differs substantially from the Ciceronian understanding of style.

A central assumption in the advent of scientific method was the belief that the human mind had sought the truth without sufficient exploration of the external world. We see this assumption expressed in William Wotton's *Reflections upon Ancient and Modern Learning*, published at the end of the seventeenth century. Wotton writes: "My Lord *Bacon* was the first great Man who took much pains to convince the World that they had hitherto been in a wrong Path, and that Nature her self, rather than her Secretaries, was to be addressed to by those who were desirous to know very much of her Mind."[14] Among Wotton's components of scientific method are:

> To collect great Numbers of Observations, and to make a vast Variety of Experiments upon all sorts of Natural Bodies. And because this cannot be done without proper Tools. . . . To contrive such Instruments, by which the Constituent Parts of the Universe, and of all its Parts, even the most minute, or the most remote, may lie more open to our View; and their Motions, or other Affections, be better calculated and examined, than could otherwise have been done by our unassisted senses. (pp. 79–80)

Human capability, then, is suspect; human judgment must be corrected by the external world, and our awareness of the world must be extended by instruments. As we move toward the twentieth century, the external world becomes even more primary and real and the human being a mere effect of it, a creature whose perceptions are misled by the vagaries of sense and mind and whose conclusions can be dismissed as opinion, illusion, or impressionism. To the greatest extent possible, researchers are eliminated from the research process and scientific instrumentation becomes even more critical, partially to minimize human error. Little wonder that impersonality has become a stylistic ideal of technical and public discourse.

Neglect of the external world was only one of the many failings that the apologists for the new science perceived in the past. Another was the disputatiousness of the rhetoricians themselves. The apologists for science denounced disputatiousness as an exercise in expression devoid of new content. Sprat complains that the scholastics "wanted matter to contrive: and so, like the *Indians*, onely express'd a wonderful Artifice, in the ordering of the same Feathers into a thousand varities of Figures."[15] Elsewhere, he claims that the Royal Society must "separate the knowledge of *Nature* from the colours of *Rhetorick*, the devices of *Fancy*, or the delightful deceit of *Fables*" (p. 12). In the province of style, these arguments promoted a serious split between form and content.

Bernard Le Bouvier de Fontenelle is typical of the apologists for science in his attack on the unintelligibility of the scholastics: "When the authority of Aristotle was unquestioned, when truth was sought only in his enigmatic writings and never in Nature, not only did philosophy not advance at all, but it fell into an abyss of nonsense and unintelligible ideas whence it was rescued only with great difficulty."[16] Wotton, influenced by Descartes's "working upon intelligible Principles in an intelligible Manner," includes intelligibility as another facet of scientific method:

> No Arguments are received as cogent, no Principles are allowed as current ... but what are in themselves intelligible; that so a Man may frame an Idea of them.... Matter and Motion with their several Qualities, are only considered in Modern Solutions of Physical Problems. *Substantial Forms, Occult Qualities, Intentional Species, Idiosyncrasies, Sympathies and Antipathies of Things*, are exploded; not because they are Terms used by Ancient Philosophers, but because they are only empty Sounds.... (pp. 300–01, 306–07)

The apologists associated not only words but also rhetorical devices with obscurity, as Sprat suggests in his most famous passage: "Who can behold ... how many mists and uncertainties, these specious *Tropes* and *Figures* have brought on our Knowledg?" The Royal Society strives

> to reject all the amplifications, digressions, and swellings of style: to return back to the primitive purity, and shortness,

> when men deliver'd so many *things*, almost in an equal number of *words*. They have exacted from all their members, a close, naked, natural way of speaking; positive expressions, clear senses; a native easiness: bringing all things as near the Mathematical plainness, as they can: and preferring the language of Artizans, Countrymen, and Merchants, before that, of Wits, or Scholars. (pp. 112–13)

The apologists, then, combine an ideal of stylistic clarity with a distrust of abstruse words and rhetorical devices.

Sprat's ideal of plainness in style stems from the preference in science for mechanism (the search for explanations of phenomena in terms of matter and motion) and for mathematics. As already noted, Wotton closely associates intelligibility with mechanism, and elsewhere he indicates that the analysis of nature in terms of matter and motion is another component of scientific method. Scientists must "adapt all the Catholick Affections of Matter and Motion to all the known Appearances of Things, so as to be able to tell how Nature works; and, in some particular Cases, to command her" (pp. 79–80). Since the abstraction of phenomena into matter and motion could only be described in mathematical terms, Wotton includes mathematics as a component of scientific method: "Mathematicks are joyned along with Physiology, not only as Helps to Men's Understandings, and Quickness of their Parts; but as absolutely necessary to the comprehending of the Oeconomy of Nature, in all her Works" (pp. 300–01). Fontenelle recommends that the mathematical approach be applied to other branches of knowledge. "The geometrical method is not so rigidly confined to geometry itself that it cannot be applied to other branches of knowledge as well. A work on politics, on morals, a piece of criticism, even a manual on public speaking would, other things being equal, be all the better for having been written by a geometrician...."[17] Researchers and practitioners who try to analyze or shape style in terms of sentence length clearly fall into this tradition. The mechanistic and mathematical approaches are attractive because they free the thinker from the imperfections and varieties of actual experience.

As Fontenelle suggests, the apologists were especially skeptical of Aristotle and other system makers. Wotton sees this skepticism as a facet of scientific method:

> Forming of Sects and Parties in Philosophy, that shall take their Denominations from, and think themselves obliged to stand by the Opinions of any particular Philosophers, is, in a manner, wholly laid aside. *Des Cartes* is not more believed

upon his own Word, than Aristotle: Matter of Fact is the only Thing appealed to; and Systems are little further regarded, than as they are proper to instruct young Beginners. . . . (pp. 300–01)

This attack on system making has its roots in Bacon's description of the "Idols of the Tribe": "The human understanding is of its own nature prone to abstractions and gives a substance and reality to things which are fleeting. But to resolve nature into abstractions is less to our purpose than to dissect her into parts. . . ."[18] Since holistic approaches in the past had been fraught with error, Bacon preferred analysis to synthesis and attention to the part over attention to the whole. This rejection of the holistic approach to experience has had a serious impact on the study of communication.

Toward the Ideal Again

Many of the stylistic reforms encouraged by the advocates of the new science were salutary. In *Science and Imagination*, Marjorie Nicolson shows us how greater attention to the physical world has enriched our language, our imagination, our emotions, and our thought.[19] Too many rhetoricians did seem caught up in argumentation and verbal games rather than in the pursuit of truth. All too often rhetorical devices did obscure the communication of matters they should have been clarifying. But the assumptions that led to both scientific method and the modern plain style have had a profoundly negative impact on communication today. Revolutions are typically reactions against excesses, and the reactions are often as excessive as the original abuses. The attempt of the new scientists to overcome the stylistic excesses of the past resulted in other excesses that must be corrected in our own age.

One of the gravest stylistic excesses of the scientific revolution was the imposition of a radical impersonality on the language of practical affairs. By the authority of experience itself—our own experience as consultants to industry—we reject impersonality as a stylistic ideal. It should not be difficult to attain impersonality in a computer manual, for example, yet we didn't read too many before tripping over an anecdote about Sherlock Holmes, of all things. In examining many computer manuals, we found a nearly universal inclination to personify the computer. We found, too, that each manual was unique, expressing somehow the personality or personalities that shaped it, no matter how inhibited the expression. A top computer company has been trying to promote what it calls "audience friendly" publications in an effort to solve the problems that arise when readers either ignore or rush through a document without interest, awareness, or understanding. In these examples we see mounting evidence that the pursuit of personality in technical discourse doesn't work. Writers strain against the obligation to write impersonal prose, and readers are bored by such prose.

The expression of personality requires a command of artistic skills, however, whose development has been discouraged by the split between form and content and the association of art with obscurity that resulted from the scientific revolution. As John Mulder indicates in *The Temple of the Mind*, students before the scientific revolution often learned to vary a theme in as many as one hundred or two hundred different ways. They strove to amplify their writing through comparison, example, description, repetition, paraphrasis, and digression.[20] Teachers before the seventeenth century, unlike almost all their counterparts today, were not afraid to drill their students in the whole range of rhetorical devices. When our own students confront writing tasks, however, they are rarely armed with sufficient tools to shape their compositions aggressively. They tend to be more concerned with what not to do than with what to do in their writing. Edward P. J. Corbett, Richard Lanham, and others have argued eloquently for the superiority of a radical innovation—the introduction of old-fashioned rhetorical devices.[21] Yet most textbooks omit even such basic stylistic techniques as antithesis, parenthesis, ellipsis, and climax. Students are expected to muddle through by stylistic instinct, an approach that reinforces the myth of the born writer.

Part of the problem lies in the view that personality is something already present, a given to be discovered rather than shaped, a message written in one's genes at the moment of conception. Louis Milic rejects the view of style as an expression of personality on exactly this basis. He rejects the theory he calls "psychological monism" because it leaves the teacher with nothing to teach; if the point of working on one's style is to express a personality, then the work will consist of trying to write more and more "naturally" (p. 69). The personality is there waiting to be let out, and consciously applied rhetorical patterns—art—would only get in the way. We would argue that such a notion of personality is at best an oversimplification. We human beings are both more and less than our genetic endowments: we are more because there are dimensions of a human being defined by culture rather than by genetics and less because we inevitably fall short of our natural capacities. Being human means *becoming* human, discovering and inventing oneself continually, both as a unique individual and as an embodiment of one's culture. We discover/invent ourselves in many media of action, but language is probably the most important. Rhetorical style expresses personality, and it can be a medium in which we become larger, more complex, more sophisticated as persons. To use rhetoric in this way, we must command the techniques of rhetorical art, the schemes and tropes and strategies of organization and argument.

What we are suggesting might be called a calculus of personality. A mathematical calculus defines the area of a curvilinear figure by inscribing in it ever more complex polygons, giving closer and closer approximations of a quantity too subtle for ultimate definition. Style articulates personality in a similar fashion. The human person is ultimately too complex for words, but through rhetorical art one achieves increasingly subtle approximations. Unlike a mathematical calculus, the act of stylistic approximation alters the figure one is aiming toward. To express one's personality in discourse is to discover or invent nuances of human being and make them part of oneself. Rhetorical devices are the techniques in this calculus of personality, and teaching them is one of the most serious educational tasks. A description of recent teaching experiments designed to introduce students to the use of rhetorical devices in technical discourse has already been published by one of us.[22]

Earlier we laid out a dilemma posed by maturity and readability as stylistic ideals. Maturity calls for longer sentences and readability for shorter sentences. If we want our students to achieve a style that is both mature and readable, we are left wondering in which syntactic direction to prod them. The dilemma arises because both stylistic ideals rest on a radical dualism; both are defined by driving a giant wedge between style and substance and then ignoring the latter. When we recognize that style cannot be abstracted so radically from substance and return to something like the Ciceronian view of style, the dilemma evaporates. Mature writers produce longer sentences because they articulate a more complex persona and a more subtle vision of reality. The readability of discourse will always be limited by its substantive complexity and sophistication. Theoretically, then, instructors should be able to teach toward a style that is both mature and readable. But to do so we must give up the quantitative precision that has made both readability and maturity quite attractive as stylistic ideals. We cannot quantify the substance of discourse.

We need not be ashamed of a rhetorical ideal that is unscientific in the sense that it cannot be characterized in abstract, quantitative terms. The tradition of classical and Renaissance rhetoric rested on concrete models to illustrate the ideal rather than on abstract characterizations of it. In the most general sense, Cicero and Demosthenes were concrete embodiments of eloquence, a concept that might be taken as the ancient equivalent of a style at once readable and mature. Specific local instances of eloquence were found in the figures of speech, and once again concrete example was of greater importance than abstract definition. In any rhetorical handbook, the definitions of these figures are maddeningly vague, but the illustrations of them are rich and pedagogically more important. The student learned the figures not by coming directly to an abstract understanding but by catching a pattern through reading and writing concrete instances.

While in one sense this pedagogy is quite unscientific, in another sense it is as scientific as the laboratory method of instruction. In *Personal Knowledge,* Michael Polanyi characterizes the method by which a scientist learns to "do science," and the process is closely analogous to the process of achieving eloquence through imitation.[23] Apprentice scientists do not learn their craft by studying a theory of the scientific method. They do experiments under the critical eye of a master. They imitate work done many times in the past, and by doing what other scientists have done they catch the pattern of scientific method. The knowledge they most need is tacit and direct rather than reflexive, the muscular understanding of an actor as contrasted with the detached intellectual understanding of a drama critic. The most able scientists will, like Polanyi, develop a detached intellectual understanding of their art and use this more philosophical knowledge to improve their work, but the philosophical understanding must rest on tacit knowledge. The stylistic art we call for likewise rests on tacit knowledge and would result from a pedagogy that employs more vigorously the tradition of imitation.

The scientific attack on systems, the preference for analysis into parts rather than synthesis of a whole, also promotes the inclination to analyze mathematically the parts of a communication situation. As in science, such analysis serves to filter out the imperfections and varieties of life as we actually experience it. But the uniqueness of any communication situation is critical to its analysis. Recall Aristotle's definition of rhetoric as the faculty of discovering in the particular case what are the available means of persuasion. Effective writers and speakers are acutely aware of all the concrete factors that bear on a specific communication situation—themselves, their audiences, their media of expression, and the constructs of reality they share with a larger community. Only one instrument has the power to analyze communication situations—the human mind. Efforts to quantify communication situations are inevitably either trivial or inconclusive because quantitative instruments will never be subtle or powerful enough for the task. The growing concern for plain language and effective communication in technology, business, and public affairs should be met by a reaffirmation of human judgment as superior to any quantitative methodology. The power and success of scientific method must not distract us from the great problems that cannot be addressed scientifically and must be addressed now.

Notes

[1] Walker Gibson, *Tough, Sweet and Stuffy: An Essay on Modern American Prose Styles* (Bloomington: Indiana Univ. Press, 1966), pp. 113–40.

[2] A good and compact overview of the literature on stylistic maturity (or syntactic fluency, a near-synonym that appears with some frequency) can be found in John C. Mellon, "Issues in the Theory and Practice of Sentence-Combining: A Twenty-Year Perspective," in *Sentence Combining and the Teaching of Writing*, ed. Donald A. Daiker, Andrew Kerek, and Max Marenberg (Conway, Ark.: L&S Books, 1979). On readability as a stylistic ideal, see E. D. Hirsch, Jr., *The Philosophy of Composition* (Chicago: Univ. of Chicago Press, 1977).

[3] Edwin Arthur Burtt, *The Metaphysical Foundations of Modern Physical Science* (1924; rpt. New York: Anchor-Doubleday, 1954), pp. 32, 79.

[4] Cicero, *Orator*, trans. H. M. Hubbell, The Loeb Classical Library (Cambridge: Harvard Univ. Press, 1962), xxiii.76; p. 363. Subsequent references to this and other works by Cicero will be to the Loeb Classical Library editions.

[5] *The Rhetoric of Aristotle*, trans. Lane Cooper (New York: Appleton, 1960), iii.12; pp. 217–19.

[6] Kenneth Burke, *Counter-Statement* (Berkeley: Univ. of California Press, 1968), p. 31.

[7] So far as we know, the distinction between these two views of the stylistic characters has not previously been noticed. In *The Art of Persuasion in Greece* (Princeton: Princeton Univ. Press, 1963), for example, George Kennedy attributes to both Aristotle and Cicero a strictly generic view (p. 280). We believe that a careful reading of the texts, particularly Chapters xxi through xxx of Cicero's *Orator*, will sustain our point. Cicero does not flatly reject the generic view, but he qualifies it importantly by adding the idea that the most skillful orators will not confine themselves to a single style in a given speech.

[8] James J. Murphy, *Rhetoric in the Middle Ages: A History of Rhetorical Theory from St. Augustine to the Renaissance* (Berkeley: Univ. of California Press, 1974), summarizes Geoffrey of Vinsauf's *Poetria Nova* (pp. 170–72) and John of Garland's *De Arte Prosayca, Metrica, et Rithmica* (pp. 177–80).

[9] On the Puritan's commitment to the plain style, see Perry Miller, *The New*

England Mind: The Seventeenth Century (Boston: Beacon, 1961), pp. 331–62.

[10] Louis T. Milic, "Theories of Style and Their Implications for the Teaching of Composition," *College Composition and Communication*, 16 (1965), 66–69, 126.

[11] For an enlightening discussion of Cicero's view of the style-substance relationship, see Raymond Di Lorenzo, "The Critique of Socrates in Cicero's *De Oratore: Ornatus* and the Nature of Wisdom," *Philosophy and Rhetoric*, 11 (1978), 247–61.

[12] Isocrates, "Antidosis," trans. George Norlin; in *Readings in Classical Rhetoric*, ed. Thomas H. Benson and Michael H. Prosser (Bloomington: Indiana Univ. Press, 1972), pp. 47–48.

[13] "Science and English Prose Style in the Third Quarter of the Seventeenth Century," in *The Seventeenth Century: Studies in the History of English Thought and Literature from Bacon to Pope* (Stanford: Stanford Univ. Press, 1951), p. 88.

[14] William Wotton, *Reflections upon Ancient and Modern Learning* (1694; rpt. Hildesheim: Georg Ohms, 1968), pp. 306–07.

[15] Thomas Sprat, *History of the Royal Society*, ed. Jackson I. Cope and Harold Whitmore Jones (St. Louis: Washington Univ. Press, 1958), pp. 15–16.

[16] "A Digression on the Ancients and the Moderns," in *The Continental Model: Selected French Critical Essays of the Seventeenth Century in English Translation*, ed. Scott Elledge and Donald Schier, rev. ed. (Ithaca, N.Y.: Cornell Univ. Press, 1970), p. 369.

[17] Taken from Paul Hazard, *The European Mind (1680–1715)*, trans. J. Lewis May (1935; rpt. Cleveland: World, 1963), p. 132.

[18] *The Works of Francis Bacon*, ed. James Spedding, Robert Leslie Ellis, and Douglas D. Heath (1870; rpt. New York: Garrett, 1968), IV, 83.

[19] Marjorie Nicolson, *Science and Imagination* (1956; rpt. Ithaca, N.Y.: Cornell Univ. Press, 1962).

[20] John Mulder, *The Temple of the Mind: Education and Literary Taste in Seventeenth-Century England* (New York: Pegasus, 1969), pp. 13–41.

[21] Edward P. J. Corbett, *Classical Rhetoric for the Modern Student* (New York: Oxford Univ. Press, 1965), includes a useful and, by modern standards, extensive treatment of figures of speech. Richard A. Lanham, *Style: An Anti-Textbook* (New Haven: Yale Univ. Press, 1974), is an eloquent and well-documented plea for revival of rhetorical play in composition classes.

[22] Merrill D. Whitburn et al., "The Plain Style in Scientific and Technical Writing," *Journal of Technical Writing and Communication*, 8 (1978), 349–58.

[23] Michael Polanyi, *Personal Knowledge: Towards a Post-Critical Philosophy* (Chicago: Univ. of Chicago Press, 1958).

7

John Locke's Contributions to Rhetoric*

EDWARD P. J. CORBETT

For many twentieth-century teachers of English, John Locke (1632–1704) is a peripheral, rather than a mainstream, figure in the literary history of the late seventeenth and early eighteenth centuries. With some of those teachers, he merits mention only as the friend and physician of the first Earl of Shaftesbury, who served as the model for Achitophel in John Dryden's famous satire, and as the tutor for the third Earl of Shaftesbury, the author of the pre-Romantic manifesto *Characteristics*. Some teachers may have read Locke's *Second Treatise on Civil Government* in connection with an undergraduate course in political science, a great books course in the humanities division, or a course on colonial American literature and learned that this document not only attempted to justify the Whig revolution of 1688 in England but also served our Founding Fathers as the rationale for our own revolution and democratic form of government. Even if they had not read snippets from Locke's *An Essay concerning Human Understanding* (1690) in anthologies of eighteenth-century literature, they could not escape the many references to that work in the literature and the literary histories of the period. If they were aware that the *Essay* was a philosophical work, they were not quite sure whether it should be classified primarily as a contribution to psychology or logic or metaphysics or epistemology. Virtually none of those twentieth-century teachers—including myself, until recently—were aware that Locke's *An Essay concerning Human Understanding* contributed to the development of rhetoric in the eighteenth century.

For those of us who regarded John Locke as only a subsidiary figure in the literary life of the eighteenth century, the following statement by Kenneth MacLean in his book *John Locke and English Literature of the Eighteenth Century* is an eye-opener:

"The book that had most influence in the Eighteenth Century, the Bible excepted, was Locke's *Essay concerning Human Understanding* (1690)."[1] And this statement by Wilbur Samuel Howell comes as quite a shocker: "*The Conduct of the Understanding* and its parent work, *An Essay concerning Human Understanding*, were without question the most popular, the most widely read, the most frequently reprinted, and the most influential, of all English books of the eighteenth century."[2] There is enough testimony of that sort now available to make unquestionable John Locke's profound effect on the intellectual life of his time, and I should like to suggest to contemporary teachers of English, especially teachers of rhetoric and composition, that Locke can give them insights into the human psyche that can enhance their teaching.

I am by no means the first one to note the rhetorical dimensions of Locke's famous *Essay*, but surprisingly little has been written about Locke as a contributor to the development of rhetorical theory. A ten-page bibliography of primary and secondary works at the back of the third edition of Richard I. Aaron's classic study contains not a single work concerning the rhetorical dimensions of Locke, if one can judge solely by the titles of the books and articles.[3] Wilbur Samuel Howell may be the first to note in a major journal that Locke influenced the development of rhetorical theory, and in a book published four years later, Howell clearly presents Locke as the dominant influence on the development of the "new logic" and the "new rhetoric" of the eighteenth century.[4]

I myself was prompted to take a look at Locke's *Essay* when I was investigating the rhetorical dimensions of John Henry Newman's *An Essay in Aid of a Grammar of Assent* (1870).[5] Newman frequently alluded to, or quoted from, Locke's *Essay*, and, while he clearly agreed with many of Locke's views on the processes of reasoning and assenting, he did disagree on a few points. So I decided to consult Locke's *Essay* to discover what might be useful for teachers in general and for teachers of writing in particular.

A convenient way for me to explore the rhetorical dimensions of the *Essay* is to make use of the six issues that Wilbur Samuel Howell saw as the main points of contention between the exponents of the old rhetoric and the exponents of the new rhetoric during the eighteenth century.[6] I will take up each issue in turn, indicate where Locke stood on the issue, and suggest some of the implications of that stand for teachers of rhetoric and composition.

(1) *Should rhetoric continue to concentrate on persuasive discourse or should it extend its province to include expository and didactic discourse?*

Rhetoric had its beginning in fifth-century Athens as the art of persuasive oratory. Throughout the next two thousand years or so, rhetoric continued to be preoccupied with persuasive discourse. Cicero and, later, Augustine tried to broaden the purview of rhetoric by positing for it a triple function: to teach (*docere*), to delight (*delectare*), and to persuade (*movere*). But it was not until the scientific revolution, brought on by individuals like Descartes, Bacon, and Newton, that the notion of the expository and didactic functions of discourse really caught on.

John Locke was infected with the scientific spirit. Not only did his own studies at Oxford lead him to become a medical doctor, but two of his closest associates at Oxford were the medical scientist Thomas Sydenham and the chemist Robert Boyle. As a member of the Royal Society, he subscribed to its proposal for the creation of a verbal style that would be suitable for the transmission of the new scientific knowledge to the general public.

Locke's view of the proper function of discourse is epitomized in the following quotation from Book III of the *Essay*, in a chapter entitled "The Abuse of Words":

> To conclude this consideration of the imperfection and abuse of language; the ends of language in our discourse with others being chiefly these three: first, to make known one man's thoughts or ideas to another; secondly, to do it with as much ease and quickness as is possible; and thirdly, thereby to convey the knowledge of things. Language is either abused or deficient when it fails in any of these three.[7]

This view of language as primarily an instrument of communication has prevailed in American composition courses in the twentieth century. Consequently, expository writing has been the dominant mode of discourse taught in the schools, although instructors have often treated argumentative writing as a species of expository writing. The notion that the language of expository discourse should be made easy to read was most recently espoused in E. D. Hirsch's plea for "relative readability."[8] The expansion of the province of rhetoric in the schools is probably due mainly to the influence of George Campbell, who proposed that the purposes of discourse were "to enlighten the understanding, to please the imagination, to move the passions, or to influence the will," or to the influence of Alexander Bain, who propagated the notion of the four modes of discourse— narration, description, exposition, and argumentation.[9] It is clear, however, that the impetus for that expansion comes from Locke's *Essay*.

(2) *Should rhetoric continue to concentrate on the so-called artistic proofs drawn from the use of the topics or should it also pursue the so-called inartistic proofs derived from outside sources?*

Locke's position on this issue is ultimately based on the thesis that he advances in Book I of the *Essay* and that becomes the major philosophical premise for his whole system of empiricism: the notion that people are born without any innate ideas.

If the human mind does not come equipped with ideas, how does it acquire knowledge? Locke answers that question in Book II. The human mind acquires all its knowledge through experience, and that experience takes two forms: sensation and reflection. The mind gets its ideas of particular, concrete objects through one of the five senses; it gets all other ideas by reflecting on its own operations. From such operations of the mind as "perception, thinking, doubting, believing, reasoning, knowing, willing," we receive into our understanding ideas as distinct as those we receive from "bodies affecting our senses" (II, i, 3–4, p. 105). To use the language of Wordsworth's "Immortality Ode," we do not come into this world "trailing clouds of glory" from some preexistent state. Rather, all our ideas come to us after birth, through the channels of our senses or through the operations of the mind on the images already perceived through the senses.

The analysis of the cognitive process as presented in Book II of the *Essay* has all kinds of implications for us as teachers. For one thing, Locke's heuristic system moves away from a reliance on classical topics and emphasizes external sources of data. Contemporary teachers have gained valuable insights into the psychology of knowing from the works of Jerome Bruner, Jean Piaget, Lev Vygotsky, and others, but we must remember that before John Locke, there were very few, if any, analyses of the dynamics of how we come to know. Locke was not endowed with any special powers of divination about the cognitive process. He merely resorted to procedures that were available to anybody from the beginning of time, namely, circumspection, retrospection, and introspection. His rather crude psychology was as remarkable for his time as Aristotle's primitive analysis of the human emotions in the *Rhetoric* was to the ancients.

Locke's analysis of how human beings imprint images on the tabula rasa of their consciousness can enlighten us teachers of composition about the potentialities and the limitations of our students' heuristic capacities. Think of the implications of a situation that Locke describes in the first chapter of Book I: "If a child were kept in a place where he never saw any other but black and white, till he were a man, he would have no more ideas of scarlet or green than he that from his childhood never tasted an oyster or a pineapple has of those particular relishes" (I.i. 6; p. 107). If our students sometimes fail in doing our writing assignments, their failure may be due, not to the malfunctioning of whatever heuristic system they may have used, but rather to the narrowly circumscribed range of their experiences. The charges frequently made about the cultural bias of some of the national intelligence tests make more sense in the light of Locke's doctrine. If we dismiss our presumption that the range of our students' sensitive and reflective experiences is fairly uniform, we may recognize the need to devise some artificial ways of helping experience-starved students catch up.

One way we can help them is to expose them to situations that can factitiously expand their reservoir of ideas either through sense perceptions or through mental reflections. Just living in the world will, of course, provide students with the kind of experiences that could enlarge their fund of knowledge. But mere exposure to experiences will not automatically enlarge that fund. Locke makes it clear that, in a sense, we have to learn how to learn. We have to attune our senses so that they will absorb, at a maximum level, the data transmitted by the big, buzzing world out there. We have to be trained to observe keenly. And of course we also have to be trained in how to reflect fruitfully. Locke puts the matter this way:

> For, though he that contemplates the operations of his mind cannot but have plain and clear ideas of them, yet unless he turn his thoughts that way and considers them *attentively*, he will no more have clear and distinct ideas of all the operations of his mind and all that may be observed therein than he will have all the particular ideas of any landscape or of the parts and motions of a clock who will not turn his eyes to it and with attention heed all the parts of it. (I.i.7; p. 107)

For that reason, as Locke observes, most children come very late to a perception of the operations of their own minds, and some never get any clear, solid ideas of these operations. The notion that our fund of ideas is dependent on the range of our experiences has at least one other implication for us teachers. If a profound disparity exists between the levels of knowledge that the speaker/writer and audience share, how can the speaker/writer achieve the kind of *identification* that Kenneth Burke says is vital for any communication and especially for persuasive discourse?[10] John H. Patton poses the problem in these words:

> If the experience of the speaker, then, is fundamentally different from the experience of the audience, the Lockian ap-

proach would not allow for the possibility of genuine communication. By Locke's analysis, cross-cultural communication for example, while not being a completely meaningless term, would yet be limited to communication based upon common experience alone. (Patton, p. 21)

Patton derives his resolution of this dilemma from the essay "Of Eloquence," in which David Hume "recalls rhetoric to its classical activity as a persuasive art in stressing two elements which had been previously discarded by Locke: passion and imagination" (Patton, p. 23). Indeed, the common ground between the rhetor and the audience may lie more in the affective realm than in the cognitive realm.

(3) *Is the structure of most rhetorical proofs fundamentally deductive or fundamentally inductive?*

From the discussion in the previous section about the importance of experience as the source of knowledge, we could guess that Locke would favor the inductive approach, and indeed he does. He does not totally reject the deductive mode of reasoning. In fact, such a rejection would have been inconsistent with his view that mathematics is the appropriate model for scientific inquiry. But in Chapter xvii of Book IV, entitled "Of Reason," he does discredit the syllogism, the Aristotelian paradigm of deductive reasoning.

His attack on the syllogism is grounded in his notion of the four degrees of reasoning:

> the first and highest is the discovering and finding out of proofs; the second, the regular and methodical disposition of them and laying them in a clear and fit order to make their connexion and force be plainly and easily perceived; the third is the perceiving their connexion; and the fourth, the making a right conclusion. (IV.xvii.3; p. 669)

Fundamentally, he contends that the syllogism applies only to the third and fourth degrees and that, even there, the syllogism was not so much a means of establishing the connections between propositions as a device for testing the connections.

If contemporary teachers of rhetoric and composition entertain an antipathy for syllogistic reasoning, they are more likely to have derived that attitude, if indirectly, from George Campbell's spirited attack on the syllogism in the sixth chapter of his *The Philosophy of Rhetoric* (1776) than from Locke's *Essay*. Regardless of the source of the current hostility or indifference to a systematic study of deductive reasoning, logic is now rarely studied formally in the composition classroom, and induction is unquestionably the reigning mode in current research and in reports on research. If any formal system of logic has replaced the scholastic logic of the syllogism in the modern composition classroom, it is symbolic logic or the claim/data/warrant system devised by Stephen Toulmin. Most college-level rhetoric texts omit any formal treatment of logic, and the few texts that do treat it devote three or four pages to a discussion of the formal and material fallacies only. In most forms of modern discourse, assertions and conclusions are more likely to be supported by empirically derived data than by deductive reasoning. Perhaps in no other area is the influence of Locke's *Essay* more evident in the modern classroom than in this shift from a reliance on deductive reasoning to a reliance on inductive reasoning.

(4) *Should rhetoric deal exclusively in probabilities or should it resort to certainties whenever they are available?*

In Book IV, Locke finally gets down to the main objective that he posed on the first page of the *Essay:* "to enquire into the original, certainty, and extent of human knowledge, together with the grounds and degrees of belief, opinion, and assent." In the first chapter of Book IV, he defined knowledge as "the perception of the connexion and agreement or disagreement and repugnancy of any of our ideas" (IV.i.2; p. 525). We come to knowledge, according to Locke, through one of three avenues: (1) through intuition, whereby we perceive the agreement or disagreement of ideas directly and immediately; (2) through demonstration, whereby we perceive their agreement or disagreement indirectly and mediately—that is, by the intervention of other ideas; and (3) through sensation (through the senses), whereby we come to an awareness of the existence of material objects. These three avenues of knowledge produce varying degrees of certainty, intuition producing the highest degree and sensation, the lowest.

In Chapter xiv of Book IV, Locke acknowledges that we would be at a great loss if we had to depend exclusively on certain knowledge in the conduct of everyday life. He recognized what Aristotle had recognized long before: that in the area of contingent human affairs, people frequently have to make practical decisions on the basis of what is only *probably* true; in fact, the situations in which our decisions can be guided by incontrovertible truths or evidence are extremely few in comparison with the many situations where we have to rely for guidance on mere probabilities.

Locke designated judgment as the faculty that helps us decide whether ideas agree or disagree when certain knowledge is not available (IV.xiv.3; p. 653). In the absence of absolute proofs, judgment relies on probabilities. Probability is the appearance of truth based on fallible proofs—that is, on proofs that lead to something less than absolute certainty (IV.xv.1; p. 654). Locke calls the acceptance that judgment accords to probable propositions "belief, assent, or opinion, which is the admitting or receiving any proposition for true upon arguments or proofs that are found to persuade us to receive it as true, without certain knowledge that it is so" (IV.xv.3; p. 655).

Up to this point, Locke does not tell us very much about probability that we could not have found in Aristotle's *Rhetoric*. For Aristotle, the area of the probable belonged to rhetoric, and the two rhetorical modes of proof, the enthymeme and the example, were distinct because they worked with probabilities and arrived at probable conclusions. In fact, the Greek word for rhetorical proofs, *pisteis*, derives from the Greek verb for "to believe." Locke made a special contribution to our views on probability by insisting on the resort to empirically verified data whenever those certainties were available, as they often are in the scientific realm. He also contributed to this matter by analyzing the psychology of assent much more extensively and intensively than Aristotle or anyone else had. Finally, he contributed to this area by proposing that there were degrees of assent, ranging "from the very neighborhood of certainty and demonstration quite down to improbability and unlikeliness, even to the confines of impossibility" (IV.xv.2; p. 655).

In the matter of degrees of assent, Locke may not have been right. Other thinkers, John Henry Newman among them, have argued that the act of assent is an all-or-nothing operation.[12] Nevertheless, Locke made a significant contribution to the teaching of rhetoric and composition by anatomizing the psychology of assent, thereby making us more conscious of the process by which assent is granted and better able to train our students in the rhetorical strategies that are likely to effect assent in a particular case.

(5) *Should discourse be organized in the six-part form recommended by Ciceronian rhetoric or could it be organized in simpler forms?*

One searches in vain in the *Essay* for any explicit pronouncement by Locke on the pattern Cicero formulated of an introduction, a narration, a partition, a proof, a refutation, and a peroration. Nor does he comment on the need for a simpler, more functional pattern of organization for modern discourse. Locke's brilliant argument in support of his thesis that we possess no innate ideas would not be difficult to analyze by means of Cicero's six-part structure. Yet from all we know about his pronouncements on other rhetorical matters, we can surmise that Locke would have approved of a simpler organizational structure, such as that recommended by Fénelon for the sermon in his *Dialogues sur l'éloquence* at the end of the seventeenth century or by Adam Smith for public addresses in his *Lectures on Rhetoric and Belles Lettres* in the mid-eighteenth century.[13] The thematic arrangement of the four books of his *Essay* is itself convincing evidence that he would not approve of the structure that the classical rhetoricians based on functions. This fifth issue is the only one requiring that we guess at the position Locke would take, but we can guess with some confidence that he would encourage the use of an organizational pattern that would facilitate the transmission of ideas to an audience of listeners or readers.

(6) *Should the rhetorical style be ornate and learned and heavily freighted with schemes and tropes or should it be plain and casual?*

As we might expect of a prominent member of the seventeenth-century Royal Society, Locke opposed the use of figurative language and other artifices of style in discourses designed to instruct and inform. In his view,

> all the art of rhetoric, besides order and clearness, all the artificial and figurative application of words eloquence has invented, are for nothing else but to insinuate wrong ideas, move the passions, and thereby mislead the judgment; and so indeed are perfect cheat. And therefore however laudable or allowable oratory may render them in harangues and popular addresses, they are certainly, in all discourses that pretend to inform and instruct, wholly to be avoided; and where truth and knowledge are concerned, cannot but be thought a great fault, either of the language or person that makes use of them. (III.x.34; p. 508)

Locke is unequivocal here in his denigration of an ornate, tendentious, and ambiguous style for certain kinds of discourse. Perry Miller has pointed out that the aim of the Royal Society, as stated in Bishop Sprat's *History of the Royal Society of London* (1667), was " 'to separate the knowledge of Nature, from the colours of Rhetorick, the devices of Fancy, or the delightful deceit of Fables.' In Locke, therefore," Miller goes on to say, "Sprat's ideal of style, freed from the domination of colors, devices, and deceits, maintaining an 'inviolable correspondence between the hand and the brain,' received at last a psychological and physiological justification."[14]

As students of English and American literature, we teachers have noted the evolution of the plain style, beginning in the eighteenth century with the casual, lucid, and graceful prose of such writers as Addison, Steele, and Swift and culminating in the twentieth century with the kind of spare, monosyllabic, short-sentence prose that Rudolf Flesch recommended highly in his *The Art of Readable Writing* (1949). We have also seen the eminently readable prose written by scientists and philosophers of the seventeenth and eighteenth centuries (Locke himself wrote that kind of prose) turn into the turgid, jargon-laden, and impersonal prose that appears in many of our professional journals. Locke can be said to have been on the winning side of this issue, and yet I think he would have agreed with those contemporary teachers of writing who deplore some of the developments in style that characterize much of the instructional and informative prose of the twentieth century.

It has been my purpose to alert teachers of rhetoric and composition to the potential usefulness of Locke's *An Essay concerning Human Understanding.* I have not attempted to point out those instances in which his exposition and defense of his views on the cognitive process may be weak or inconsistent or downright wrong. Only a seasoned philosopher could detect the soft spots in Locke's position or presentation. One of the most judicious assessments of the strengths and weaknesses of Locke's views is provided by D. J. O'Connor, Professor of Philosophy at the University of Exeter, in his book entitled simply *John Locke.*[15] But on the chance that I have succeeded in arousing the interest of some teachers, I would hasten to add that Locke's *Essay* should not be made required reading for undergraduate students in our composition courses. Rather, we teachers should read and ponder it so that we can appropriate from it, and relay to our students, what could help them to understand how they come to know what they know and how they can effectively communicate to others what they have learned.

Locke himself would not approve of our using his book to teach rhetoric. Although he served in 1663 as Lecturer in Rhetoric at Christ Church, Oxford, he disapproved of formal classroom instruction in rhetoric, preferring instruction by example rather than by precept and by tutoring rather than by lecturing.[16] But he would approve of our consulting his book to learn something about how human beings think. In a paper, "Reading and Study," that he wrote in 1703, a year before his death, he said that it was imperative for us to acquire "a knowledge of men," and he strongly recommended the reading of "books that of purpose treat of human nature, which help to give an insight into it. Such are those treating of the passions, and how they are moved, whereof Aristotle in his second book of *Rhetoric* hath admirably discoursed, and that in a little compass."[17] Although Locke did not himself discourse in a "little compass," he did give us one of those books that supply the kind of knowledge about the cognitive behavior of men and women so vital to the rhetorician.

Notes

* A slightly different version of this article was published in *College Composition and Communication*, 32 (Dec. 1981).

1 Kenneth MacLean, *John Locke and English Literature of the Eighteenth Century* (New Haven: Yale Univ. Press, 1936), p. v.

2 Wilbur Samuel Howell, *Eighteenth-Century British Logic and Rhetoric* (Princeton: Princeton Univ. Press, 1971), p. 277.

3 Richard I. Aaron, *John Locke* (Oxford: Clarendon, 1971).

4 Wilbur Samuel Howell, "John Locke and the New Rhetoric," *Quarterly Journal of Speech*, 53 (1967) 319–33. John B. O'Hara did a Ph.D. dissertation entitled "John Locke's Philosophy of Discourse" at the University of Oklahoma in 1963, and Jerry L. Weedon did a Ph.D. dissertation entitled "Philosophy as a Rationale for Rhetorical Systems: A Case Study Derivation of Rhetorical Cognates from the Philosophical Doctrines of John Locke" at UCLA in 1969. There have also been some additional articles published on Locke's contributions to rhetoric since Howell's article appeared in 1967: Jerry L. Weedon, "Locke on Rhetoric and Rational Man," *Quarterly Journal of Speech*, 56 (1970), 378–87; L. Brooks Hill, "Lockeian Influences in the Evolution of Rhetorical Theory," *Central States Speech Journal*, 26 (1975), 107–14; John H. Patton, "Experience and Imagination: Approaches to Rhetoric by John Locke and David Hume," *Southern Speech Communication Journal*, 41 (1975), 11–29.

5 See Edward P. J. Corbett, "Some Rhetorical Lessons from John Henry Newman," *College Composition and Communication*, 31 (1980), 402–12.

6 The six issues are listed and elaborated on in Howell's *Eighteenth-Century British Logic and Rhetoric*, pp. 441–47. I have paraphrased Howell's statements of the issues.

7 John Locke, *An Essay concerning Human Understanding*, ed. Peter H. Nidditch (Oxford: Clarendon, 1979), p. 504. Hereafter citations from the *Essay* will be documented parenthetically in the text with a notation like this: III.x.23; p. 504—that is, Book III, Chapter x, paragraph 23, on p. 504 of the Nidditch edition. I have made changes in Locke's style of capitalizing, italicizing, spelling, and punctuating whenever I felt that those features would puzzle or distract my readers.

8 E. D. Hirsch, *The Philosophy of Composition* (Chicago: Univ. of Chicago Press, 1977).

9 George Campbell, *The Philosophy of Rhetoric* (1776), ed. Lloyd F. Bitzer (Carbondale: Southern Illinois Univ. Press, 1963), p. 1; Alexander Bain, *English Composition and Rhetoric* (New York: Appleton, 1866).

10 Kenneth Burke, *A Rhetoric of Motives* (Berkeley: Univ. of California Press, 1969), p. 55.

11 Those who are interested in a more detailed summary of Locke's attack on

the Syllogism can consult pp. 285–89 of Wilbur Samuel Howell's *Eighteenth-Century British Logic and Rhetoric.*

[12] John Henry Newman, *An Essay in Aid of a Grammar of Assent,* ed. Charles Frederick Harrold (London: Longmans, 1947), pp. 131–33. In a lecture entitled "A Comparison of John Locke and John Henry Newman on the Rhetoric of Assent," given at the Speech Communication Association Convention, Anaheim, California, 12 November 1981, I argued that Newman was right and Locke wrong in the matter of degrees of assent.

[13] For a convenient summary of Fénelon's and Adam Smith's recommendations about arrangement, see Howell, *Eighteenth-Century British Logic and Rhetoric,* pp. 446, 572.

[14] Perry Miller, "The Rhetoric of Sensation," in *Perspectives of Criticism,* ed. Harry T. Levin (Cambridge: Harvard Univ. Press, 1950), p. 106.

[15] O'Connor's book was originally published in 1952 in the Pelican Philosophy Series and was reissued with minor changes in 1967 in the Dover Publications Series on Philosophy.

[16] See Maurice Cranston, *John Locke: A Biography* (London: Longmans, 1957), pp. 20–21, 25.

[17] Cranston, p. 245.

8

Rhetoric in the Liberal Arts: Nineteenth-Century Scottish Universities

WINIFRED BRYAN HORNER

In the Scottish universities of the nineteenth century, there existed a deep concern for democratic and humanistic values, and, through that concern, Scottish education shared a bond with American and Continental universities of the period. Out of that concern came a strong commitment to a liberal arts education designed to provide a broad preparation not only for those students who might later wish to specialize in theology, law, or medicine but also for those who did not choose to pursue a profession. The primary purpose of this form of education was to produce the informed citizenry deemed essential to the health of democratic nations. Above all, such basic education was intended to be open to all. Although the United States still holds to that commitment, at least ostensibly, education in England does not and never has. For the English, such education has always been for the well-born, the well-bred, the elite.

This commitment to a democratic form of education entails responsibilities and creates problems for which there are no simple or easy solutions. During the nineteenth century, the four Scottish universities—St. Andrews, Glasgow, Edinburgh, and Aberdeen—faced those responsibilities and encountered problems much like the ones encountered by American universities today. Issues were enjoined and solutions proposed. The validity of the lecture system versus a program of instruction in philosophy and rhetoric that emphasized discussion and theme writing was disputed. Liberal arts versus specialization and classical studies versus studies in English were also at issue. These controversies developed out of deep philosophical disagreements.

The history of the Scottish universities in the eighteenth and nineteenth centuries is closely connected with the sixty-year Scottish resistance to the southern, or English, encroachment. In the 1707 Act

of Union that joined Scotland to England, the Scots gave up their political and economic freedom but fiercely kept their independence in
the areas of religion, law, and education. During the eighteenth century, religion and law succumbed to English pressures, but Scottish
education fought to retain its remarkably philosophic and democratic
flavor. While learning in England was class-conscious and confined
to the few, many Scots had access to education. During the nineteenth century, the defense of this educational philosophy became
for many Scots a kind of nationalism, the chief form of resistance to
English domination.

In the eighteenth and nineteenth centuries, the four Scottish
universities were a great source of national pride. Highly innovative,
they pioneered in studies that are now a part of contemporary curricula. Newton's theories were first taught at the northern universities, and German philosophy, economics, and agriculture were a
regular part of the curricula at Edinburgh and Glasgow. Medicine
was introduced as an academic discipline at these universities long
before Oxford and Cambridge took it up. And the study of English
literature was established early in the north, while Oxford and Cambridge were concentrating only on Greek and Latin. English literature was considered part of the folk literature or vernacular and was
therefore unworthy of serious study, an attitude much like the one
that we find in modern American universities toward black, Chicano,
Indian, and women's studies. Cambridge did not introduce its first
course in English literature until 1904, while chairs of English literature were established in Edinburgh in 1845 and at Harvard in 1876.

This development shows that these two universities had similar goals and that the two countries in which they were located had
similar commitments to education. William Edmonstone Aytoun, the
first professor of English literature at Edinburgh, and Francis J.
Child, the first professor of English at Harvard, are best known today as collectors of ballads. Aytoun's collection of Scottish ballads is
still the standard, as Child's is of the English ballads. These first professors of English literature both came to their teaching as rhetoricians who loved the language and literature of the common people,
ordinarily referred to in the nineteenth century as folk-poetry, in contrast to art-poetry. More important, both professors came out of
strongly democratic traditions.

Fashioned after the Italian and French models, the democratic mode of education at the Scottish universities was quite different from that of their counterparts in England and Germany at the
beginning of the nineteenth century. First, the Scottish universities
did not have compulsory entrance exams before 1889, and students
arrived at the universities at a young age. At Aberdeen in 1827, the

average age of the entering students was thirteen, while at St. Andrews, Edinburgh, and Glasgow, the age was between fourteen and sixteen. Scottish lower schools were few and varied in quality, and students were not only young but often ill prepared when they came to the universities. Many Scottish districts could not provide adequate preparatory education, and the universities took that responsibility.

Entering students embarked on a four-year general curriculum centered on a philosophy-arts program that emphasized rhetoric and writing. The 1844 calendar of the University of Glasgow lists five professors in the Faculty of Arts: humanity, Greek, logic, moral philosophy, and natural philosophy. These professors presided over the "Gowned Classes," and students enrolled in one or two courses a session. Students were required by the "complete academic course enjoined by the ancient usage of the University" to attend classes regularly for four years. In England, however, only the best prepared and brightest students were admitted to the universities, and the rhetoric- and philosophy-oriented general program had beén replaced by highly specialized curricula. The English student had only two options: classical studies at Oxford and mathematics at Cambridge. In Scotland, it was only after the initial arts program that the student went on to study a specialty. Many students never went beyond the initial program.

When Dr. Johnson, never an admirer of the Scots, criticized their universities for being superficial, Francis Jeffrey defended the Scottish system:

> I endorse, on the whole the justice of the reproach that has been levelled against our general national instruction—that our knowledge, though more general, is more superficial than with our neighbours. That is quite true, and our system leads to it, but I think it is a great good on the whole, because it enables relatively large numbers of people to get—not indeed profound learning, for that is not to be spoken of—but that knowledge which tends to liberalise and make intelligent the mass of our population, more than anything else.[1]

An important champion of the Scottish system was George Jardine, Professor of Logic and Rhetoric at the University of Glasgow from 1774 to 1827. During his long tenure, he was deeply involved in the major educational issues of the day: the validity of liberal arts versus specialization and of instruction in the classics versus instruction in English. He also supported rhetoric, discussion, and writing as a way of learning in conjunction with lectures. Although his name may be unfamiliar to us, his ideas were preserved in his students' notes and in his book *Outlines of Philosophical Education*, first published at the University Press in Glasgow in 1818 and reprinted in 1825.[2]

Jardine supported the idea on which the University of Glasgow was founded; he regarded the arts, not as vocational training, but as a preparation for later specialization. He recognized the differences between the English system of education and the Scottish one:

> So great indeed is the difference in the means and system of instruction adopted in the several universities of Great Britain, that it might, for a moment, appear doubtful, whether the minds to be cultivated were really of the same order, and the professional qualifications to be attained had any thing in common. (pp. 415–16)

Jardine argues that a plan of education should be formed "according to the state of knowledge, and the prevailing pursuits of the period in which it originates." While the purpose of Greek education was to qualify young men to become "good members of the commonwealth," Roman education was to prepare youth "for the business of the senate and of the bar" (pp. 415–16). Education in the Middle Ages aimed to prepare candidates for service to the church, while Scottish education, according to Jardine, should be designed for "young men destined to fill various and very different situations in life," to allow them "to comprehend the elements of those other branches of knowledge, upon which the investigation of science, and the successful despatch of business, are found chiefly to depend" (p. 31). Jardine, however, knew that knowledge in itself was not enough, and he admonished his students: "A man may be capable of great reflections but if he cannot communicate it to others, it can be of but little use."[3] He felt that rhetoric in its fullest sense was central to the Scottish arts program.

Jardine also questioned the emphasis on Greek and Latin in the English universities: "We do not, in this part of the kingdom, attach to classical learning that high and almost exclusive degree of importance which is ascribed to it elsewhere" (p. 418). According to Jardine, the practice of delivering in Latin the lectures of the first philosophy class was continued until 1750

> when Adam Smith was appointed professor of logic; and, being rather unexpectedly called to discharge the duties of his office, he found it necessary to read to his pupils, in the English language, a course of lectures on rhetoric and belles lettres, which he had formerly delivered in Edinburgh. (p. 20)

Adam Smith's successor followed Smith's lead, and most lectures in the Scottish universities were delivered in English after that date. English had become the language of instruction by the middle of the eighteenth century, and English literature a legitimate subject of study by the middle of the nineteenth century.

The most important issue for Jardine, however, and an issue of special interest today, concerned the lecture system of the Scottish universities. In *Outlines of Philosophical Education*, Jardine urged discussion sessions and regular writing exercises beyond the daily lecture. By taking this stand, he opposed not the English system, which was largely tutorial, but the prevailing practice at the other Scottish universities, where most instruction was solely by lecture:

> It is with reluctance I repeat the remark, that, in several of our academical establishments, the philosophical education of youth is very imperfectly understood, and most inefficiently conducted. The exertion, whatever it may be, is almost entirely confined to the professor. The pupils are not required to do any thing. It is pretty much left to themselves whether they shall be utterly idle or partially employed, whether they shall derive any advantage from their attendance on the lecture, or go away, at the end of the course, as ignorant and uninformed as when it began. Surely, the common sense of the nation will not much longer permit such an abuse of the means of improvement. (pp. 523–24)

Jardine emphasized discussion hours, or the catechetical system, accompanied by theme writing in all classes. According to the statutes of the University of Glasgow, all professors, in addition to their morning lectures, were required to hold class hours during the morning for the purpose of examining their students and assigning writing exercises. Jardine kept his students for an additional hour each day so that they could discuss the lectures and read or report on themes that had been assigned.

No one was more aware of the problems inherent in such a system than Jardine himself. He was the first to acknowledge that it created extra work for the professor; he admitted that "this system of practical instruction is much more difficult than the composition of lectures" (p. 293). He recognized that assigning a large number of themes was an added burden in classes that sometimes numbered two hundred students. He suggested, however, that the system was particularly necessary in the Scottish universities, where there were many students "who are not qualified, either in respect of age or of previous acquirements" (p. 427).

The problems that Jardine encountered sound familiar, and his solutions are enlightening for teachers of writing at the college level today who face large classes and inadequately prepared students. His lecture review through discussion and writing, his sequenced assignments, and his methods of theme reading and evaluation were designed not only to instruct students in basic writing but also to allow the professor to work with large numbers of written assignments.

During the first hour of the examination period, the professor quizzed the students on the content of the lecture. The purpose of the questions, Jardine asserts, is "to bring from them [the students] the knowledge they have acquired by the lecture, expressed in their own manner." But he warns that "the same questions cannot be put indiscriminately." Some students may have no trouble answering the questions, but "there are many who, from inattention, defect of memory, or want of intellect . . . require that hints should be supplied to aid their recollection" (p. 282). He adds that the professor should proceed with "kindness and affability" with those students who "cannot overcome the embarrassment into which they are thrown by their natural timidity" (p. 282). In citing the advantages of the discussion hour, Jardine concludes by advising the instructor that

> he may frequently seize a favourable opportunity for rousing the indolent, for encouraging the diffident, for directing the spirit of the adventurous, and for bringing down the pretensions of the petulant and the assuming. (p. 285)

During the second part of the discussion hour, Jardine instructed his students "to produce an abridgment in writing of all they have heard in the morning—the order, the method, the principal topics, and the illustrations—as far as they can recollect them" (p. 287). After the students have finished this exercise, they are called on "indiscriminately and at random" to read portions of their writing. As an alternative to this writing exercise, a professor might ask some students to draw up an abridgment of the lecture while the others engage in discussion, teaching the art of "excluding the distracting influence of external objects" (p. 288). Jardine asserts that this exercise combines different activities of the mind: "The students have to remember,—to select and arrange the materials furnished to them, and to express, on the spur of the occasion, their ideas in plain and perspicuous language" (pp. 289–90).

In assigning themes, Jardine recognizes the necessity of ordering the assignments in degree of difficulty as the session progresses. The themes assigned during the first two months of the session are based on the lectures. These themes, assigned almost every day, are to be written at night and read in class the next day. The object for the student is "to form clearer and more accurate notions of the subjects discussed in the lectures than can be acquired from merely hearing them delivered" as well as accustoming the student "to express his thoughts on these subjects in correct and perspicuous language" (p. 297).

The second order of themes requires the student "to cultivate the faculties, whose office it is to arrange and classify the subjects of our knowledge, according to their nature and relations" (p. 303). Jardine gives examples of possible topics: "How may the books in a library be arranged, according to a natural or an artificial classification?" or "In what way may the whole words of a language be brought under certain classes?" (p. 305).

The third order of themes requires the student "to judge and reason for himself" (p. 307). Jardine's lectures furnished full directions for the exercise of reason and judgment and were supplemented by readings. But he saw reason and communication as closely allied:

> The faculty of reason and of speech depend greatly on, and assist each other. It is the faculty of reasoning which leads us to use the faculty of communication, and the latter faculty exists in improving the former. The faculty of reason and speech therefore have a reciprocal effect on each other.[4]

Suggested topics for the third order of themes include "Is the institution of prizes in universities useful?" "Do holidays promote study?" "Whether a town or a country life is most favourable to study?" Jardine acknowledges that not all students have sufficient knowledge to write on such subjects. He recognizes, however, the value of prewriting and drafts and the concept of writing as process: "In all cases, perfect specimens must be preceded by many unsuccessful efforts." But these efforts are "the natural and indispensable steps which lead to higher degrees of perfection," especially when "properly submitted to as to a teacher, who can direct how they may be rendered more complete." Jardine offers, in this connection, a cogent bit of advice for student writers:

> Besides, it is abundantly obvious, that if a young man did not begin to compose on any subject till he had obtained a complete knowledge of it, he would never begin at all, and the

season of forming that important habit would be utterly lost. (p. 313)

The fourth and final order of themes leads the student "to improve those faculties of the mind which are employed in the higher processes of investigation" (p. 322). Jardine demonstrates that these exercises are to improve "the powers of attention, discrimination, and investigation—to conduct the mind from phenomena to causes, from particular to general truths, and thus to produce habits of reasoning which may easily be applied to other subjects" (p. 328). Finally, Jardine advises that students should occasionally be allowed to choose their own subjects for themes. "Rules prevent deviations and irregularities, but they can never create inventions, or lead to higher degrees of excellence." He adds "that the noblest works of genius have not been the result of precept." Therefore, he urges that young persons should be allowed on occasion "to make bold attempts, to disdain the little limits of their reign" (p. 352), but he adds a precaution that students should be "required to subjoin a signed declaration to their theme, that it is their own composition, and not copied or altered from any author" (p. 353). Jardine further warns that themes must be "prescribed frequently and regularly" and that the subjects must also be various and numerous.

> Were the same topics given out every succeeding session, there would be a great risk of idle and negligent students borrowing and copying those of a former year, and even attentive students might occasionally have recourse to such performances to abridge their labour. In this case, themes, like the strings of syllogisms, formerly well known in some celebrated seminaries, would become a sort of college property, descending from one generation to another. (p. 294)

For determining the merits of themes, Jardine devises a process designed not only to aid the student but also to alleviate some of the burden of the professor. He admits that the time and labor required to examine the themes of a class might at first appear "considerable" but that "experience and habit enable the teacher to execute this work more expeditiously than might at first sight be believed" (p. 364). While the instructor cannot possibly examine all the papers, he should examine them regularly or bring them "to public notice." For the students whose exercises are overlooked will "become relaxed, their spirits depressed, and their feelings irritated. . . . If our essays pass without notice, they naturally ask, why need we give ourselves so much trouble in composing them?" (p. 367). He suggests that the first class of themes should be read aloud to the class and that the professor can at that time make appropriate remarks. Or, as an alternative, the professor himself can mark the papers at home and then read some of them aloud the following day, commenting on general defects or merits. Jardine urges the instructor not to "give offence" in the exposure of defects, "a matter of considerable delicacy" (p. 365). He acknowledges the difficulty of dealing with the treatment of the "more faulty exercises.... Were he to expose them in the unqualified terms of dissapprobation which they may possibly deserve, he might ruin every chance of being useful to their authors." So he advises the instructor to overlook some of these first faults while "neglecting no opportunity of encouraging the student to do better" (p. 366).

For the second and third order of themes, Jardine suggests appointing ten or twelve of the best students to serve as "examinators," but he lays down strict rules for these examinators. First, they are expressly prohibited from discussing the themes with other students. Second, they are to begin by reading the whole theme in order to understand its general outline. Third, they are instructed not merely to point out defects but also to select those parts of the essay that deserve to be read in class. Fourth, the examinators must couch their criticisms in "liberal and becoming terms" (p. 370). Finally, the examinators, as well as the other students in the class, must never mention outside the classroom any criticisms that have been made about the essays. A violation of any one of these rules would result in immediate dismissal from the class.

Recognizing the power and efficacy of peer evaluation, Jardine suggests "the idea of extending to every one, in his turn, an opportunity for exercising his powers of criticism" (p. 371). Finally, Jardine introduced into the arts curriculum the awarding of prizes for themes, which were to be judged by the students themselves.

> It may be imagined, at first view, that the office of judge would be best performed by the professor; but, after long experience, and much attention to the subject in all its bearings, I am inclined to give a decided preference to the exercise of this right as vested in the students. (p. 385)

This program, developed nearly one hundred and fifty years ago, was ideal in serving the needs of a democratic nation. It furnished a broad liberal arts education for all the citizens, and Jardine and his colleagues saw a full rhetoric—the ability to reason, to investigate, to judge, to write, and to speak—as an integral part of that education. Although Jardine had never heard phrases such as "peer evaluation," "writing as discovery," "writing across the curriculum," and "writing as process," he was quite familiar with the concepts.

Unfortunately, Jardine waged a losing battle against the English domination of the Scottish universities. The system he supported was under constant attack and was finally abolished by the Royal Commission in 1889. The stiff entrance examinations that were instituted forced instruction in writing and rhetoric to the secondary level. Thereafter the doors were closed to young people from the outlying districts, and the democratic and humanistic general education that had typified the Scottish universities was abandoned. Higher education became specialized and exclusive, as it still is.

Today, education in the United States is committed to the same values as those of the nineteenth-century Scottish universities, best exemplified by George Jardine. This education includes a liberal arts program open to all students and considered a prerequisite to the study of medicine, engineering, and business. When humanists fail to take seriously the general liberal arts part of their educational program and fail to see rhetoric as the heart of the arts education, they abrogate their commitment to democracy. When they fail to see the ability to reason, to read, to write, and to communicate as a skill vital to a democratic society, not only is their commitment to democracy empty but democracy itself stands in imminent peril.

Notes

1 George Elder Davie, *The Democratic Intellect: Scotland and Her Universities in the Nineteenth Century* (Edinburgh: Univ. Press, 1961), p. 27.
2 George Jardine, *Outlines of Philosophical Education Illustrated by the Method of Teaching the Logic Class in the University of Glasgow* (Glasgow: Univ. Press, 1825). All further references to this work will be in the text.
3 Notes from Jardine's lectures on logic taken by George Palmes, 1793–94, MS. Gen. 737, Glasgow Univ. Library, II, 157.
4 Notes, MS. Gen. 737, II, 155–56.

9

Nineteenth-Century Psychology and the Shaping of Alexander Bain's *English Composition and Rhetoric*

GERALD P. MULDERIG

The concept of the paragraph as a short unit of writing focused by a topic sentence and developed according to such principles as unity, coherence, and emphasis has been a staple of twentieth-century composition courses.[1] But despite the currency that this model has enjoyed, it did not arrive in the modern composition classroom trailing clouds of glory from the ancient tradition of rhetoric. Instead, this notion of the paragraph is generally regarded as having originated only a century ago in the work of Alexander Bain (1818–1903), professor of logic and rhetoric at the University of Aberdeen from 1860 to 1880.[2] Bain's influential *English Composition and Rhetoric: A Manual*, published in 1866 for use in his own composition courses, laid out six "rules" for writing paragraphs that were repeated in other nineteenth-century texts and have lived on in only slightly different form in the twentieth century. Looking back in 1894 on Bain's accomplishments as a rhetorician, Edwin Lewis commented glowingly that the paragraph rules "were illustrated and defended with the same acuteness and grasp that have made Bain perhaps the ablest writer on rhetoric since Aristotle."[3]

That is high praise for a man whose major interests and publications lay outside the field of rhetoric. Bain's first love, and the discipline to which he devoted most of his energy, was psychology; his major works, in fact, mark the culmination of association psychology, which emphasizes the principles that determine the sequences of mental phenomena. Bain's autobiography reveals little about his interior life, but it does offer some glimpses into the growth of his fascination with this field of study. After only a year as a student at Marischal College in 1837, Bain found his earlier interest in mathematics completely supplanted by his curiosity about mental processes, the study of which he notes "had now become with me incessant and overmastering."[4] Later, bored by his moral philosophy course, Bain would sit in class silently analyzing the flow of his thoughts and trying to account for the links between them. When he attempted a similar analysis with samples of writing, he became so excited by the project that he had to go off to the country for three days in order to "quiet the nervous ebullition" (*Autobiography*, pp. 75–76). By 1849 Bain had formulated the ideas that provided the basis for the first part of his great psychological treatise, *The Senses and the Intellect*, which was published in 1855. Part II, *The Emotions and the Will*, appeared four years later. With their emphasis on the links between psychology and physiology, these two books radically changed the field. As Bain's most recent editor, Daniel N. Robinson, puts it: "For a half-century, Bain's volumes *were* psychology in the English-speaking world. Perhaps no other texts, not even those by James, were as singularly effective in giving direction to psychological inquiry."[5]

It should not surprise us to discover that Bain's psychological research influenced his rhetorical theory, particularly since he wrote his *Rhetoric* during the same years in which he was engaged in preparing new editions of both psychology texts.[6] Of course, Bain was not the first rhetorician to consider psychological theories, which in one form or another have been at the heart of writing on rhetoric for 2,500 years. But because Bain was a professional psychologist—and, more than that, a major figure in the field—his applications of psychology to rhetoric deserve special attention. Two sections of Bain's *Rhetoric*—his discussion of figures of speech and his analysis of persuasion based on emotional appeals—strikingly illustrate this early attempt to bring a major fund of psychological data to bear on the shaping of a rhetorical theory.

Like many other nineteenth-century rhetorics, Bain's text gives prominence to style, beginning, in fact, with the customary classification of figures of speech. In an important way, though, Bain's opening section is unconventional. In his autobiography he writes, without explanation, that he gave "an entirely new turn to the classification [of figures]" (p. 278). This "new turn" is provided by associationist principles of epistemology as Bain presents them in his first psychology text.

In *The Senses and the Intellect,* Bain describes human thought as the product of three intellectual properties—discrimination, retentiveness, and agreement. Discrimination, the most fundamental, operates according to the principle of relativity or contrast. "By this is meant," Bain writes, "that, as change of impression is an indispensable condition of our being conscious, ... every mental experience is necessarily *twofold"* (*Senses and Intellect,* p. 8). We recognize heat, Bain explains, only because we have known cold; we appreciate leisure or rest because it contrasts with exertion. In fact, all knowledge depends on the mind's ability to recognize two contrasting things simultaneously. "[T]he principle of Relativity," he writes, "applies to everything that we are capable of knowing. Whatever we can conceive implies some other thing or things also conceivable, the contrast, co-relative, or negative of that" (*Senses and Intellect,* p. 9).

But such mental contrasts would be impossible without the mind's second property, retentiveness, which enables us to retain or to recover impressions after their source has been withdrawn. Retentiveness, the basis of memory and habit, operates by the principle of contiguity, the cohering tendency displayed by sensations that have occurred simultaneously in the mind. As Bain puts it, "Impressions that have frequently accompanied one another in the mind grow together, so as to become at last almost inseparable: we cannot have one without a disposition or prompting to renew all the rest" (*Senses and Intellect,* p. 324).

Like retentiveness, the mind's third property, agreement, is a source of what Bain calls "mental *reproduction"* (*Senses and Intellect,* p. 325). The principle of contiguity links impressions related by their simultaneous occurrence in the mind; but the principle of similarity, which directs agreement, connects impressions that were previously unassociated, enabling us to perceive resemblances and thus to order our otherwise random impressions of the world. Through it we are able to experience "a certain shock or start,—the shock of recognition; which is all the greater according as the circumstances of the present and of the past occurrence are different" (*Senses and Intellect,* p. 324).

Bain did not invent the psychological principles of contrast, contiguity, and similarity, which date back in similar form to Aristotle. But in his *English Composition and Rhetoric* he found an application for them that sets this composition text apart from others published at midcentury. Observing at the start of the *Rhetoric* that "[s]everal of the more important Figures [of speech] have reference to the operations of the human Understanding, or Intellect, and may be classified accordingly," Bain introduces the mental properties of discrimination, retentiveness, and agreement as the framework for his classification. Under the property of discrimination he places figures of antithesis, under retentiveness come metonymy and synecdoche, and under agreement we find simile, metaphor, personification, and allegory (pp. 2–3).[7] The arrangement is not simply ornamental. For Bain, it provides a way of using association psychology to explain how figures of speech acquire their rhetorical effectiveness and to suggest how they are generated.

Bain's discussion begins with agreement, or similarity, which he calls "most fruitful in figures." Echoing his discussion of "mental reproduction" in *The Senses and the Intellect*, Bain describes similarity as "the chief inventive power of the mind," which creates links between new sensations and related old ones. Figures of similarity, Bain suggests, enable the rhetorician to move readers by triggering their mental powers of agreement. Such figures may be used to appeal to the understanding, by clarifying a subject, or to the feelings, by giving "greater intensity or impressiveness to the meaning" (*Rhetoric*, pp. 3, 5). But even when a similitude accomplishes neither of these ends, it may still inspire in the reader what Bain called in his psychology text the "shock of recognition." "A comparison that is new and not obvious," he writes in the *Rhetoric*, "strikes us with a pleasurable flash, even although contributing little, either to elucidate a subject, or to excite livelier feelings in connexion with it" (p. 6).

The figures of contiguity—metonymy and synecdoche—function similarly. In *The Senses and the Intellect*, Bain illustrated the principle of contiguity by noting that "one medium of the restoration to consciousness of a particular past state, is the actual presence of some impression that had often occurred *in company* with that state. Thus we are reminded of a *name*—as ship, star, tree—by seeing the *thing;* the previous concurrence of name and thing has led to a mental companionship between the two" (p. 324). In the *Rhetoric* he introduces figures of contiguity in similar terms, describing them as rooted in the mind's natural operations:

> Now, the chief way that retentiveness or memory works is this: impressions *occurring together*, become associated together, as sunrise with daylight; and when we are made to think of one, we are reminded of the accompaniments. . . . Hence, the mental association of things *contiguously* placed, is a prominent fact of our mind; and one of its many consequences is to cause us often to name a thing by some of its adjuncts, as "the throne" for the sovereign, "gold" for wealth. Such is the nature of the *Metonymy.* (p. 3)

In his discussion of figures of contrast, Bain again links both the generation and use of figures of speech with psychological principles. As in *The Senses and the Intellect*, he explains that change of impression is "a first principle of the human mind" (p. 24). Figures such as antithesis simply make explicit in language the contrasts that are central to human cognition. In Bain's words:

> The essential plurality of Knowledge is not fully represented in ordinary language, which usually provides only one name for one subject of discourse, as heat, man, wisdom. We are supposed to be capable of recalling the full contrast involved in each case—heat as against *cold*, man—*brute*, &c. Still, it not unfrequently happens that our understanding of a thing is aided by the express mention of the contrasting things; this mention is therefore a device of Rhetoric; and to it are applied the designations, Antithesis and Contrast. (p. 25)

Bain's classification system is not quite so neat as this summary suggests; it left him no place for eight other figures—epigram, hyperbole, climax, interrogation, exclamation, apostrophe, innuendo, and irony—that had to be added somewhat awkwardly at the end. One must admit, moreover, that it is difficult to see how such a classification system might have practical value for a writer. But these facts should not diminish Bain's accomplishment. His psychological explanation of the way figures of speech work was convincing enough to influence discussions about such figures for the remainder of the nineteenth century.[8] And his conclusions cannot be dismissed as irrelevant in the twentieth century. By suggesting that figures of speech are merely formulations in language of the mind's natural processes, Bain anticipated Frank D'Angelo's recent comment that the rhetorician must "relate the structure of thought to the structure of discourse."[9] Though incomplete, Bain's observations are a form of what D'Angelo has called a conceptual theory of rhetoric.

The most thorough application of Bain's association psychology to rhetoric occurs in his chapter on persuasion, which is longer than any of the other chapters devoted to the forms of discourse and in Bain's own view the most classical. "It was the branch of Oratory or Persuasion," he wrote in his autobiography, "that brought into the foreground the more valuable and ambitious portion of the ancient rhetoric" (p. 279). Indeed, Aristotle's mark on this chapter is clear. When Bain classifies the types of persuasion as "The Oratory of the Law Courts," "Political Oratory," "Pulpit Oratory," and "Moral Suasion," he is simply adapting the deliberative, forensic, and epideictic rhetoric. Like Aristotle, Bain insists on the importance of knowing one's subject and audience thoroughly. And although he deals only briefly with ethical proof, Bain follows Aristotle in giving prominence to two other kinds of persuasion, persuasion by argument and by emotion. It is to this latter category, persuasion by emotional appeals, that Bain brings his research as a psychologist. The three types of emotional appeals described in the *Rhetoric* are all firmly grounded in his second psychological treatise, *The Emotions and the Will.*

This work stresses the link between feeling and volition that Bain sees as fundamental to human nature. In his view, our "volitional education" begins with the earliest spontaneous movements we make to sustain feelings of pleasure or to alleviate pain. Gradually, through the mind's power of retentiveness, the connections between stimuli of pleasure or pain and willed action are cemented, so that "there is at the bottom of every genuine voluntary impulse, some one variety of the many forms wherein pain or pleasure takes possession of the conscious mind" (*Emotions and Will*, pp. 310–11, 356).

Between stimulus and willed action, though, is another psychological operation, one that gives us confidence that the action we take will have the effect we desire. What, Bain asks, provokes us to lift a cup of water to our lips when we are thirsty, an action that does not in itself alleviate our thirst? Such an impulse, he explains, "must be sustained by something else than the feeling of pain relieved, for as yet no such feeling comes of [it]." This sustaining power, "arising more or less as a result of experience," is belief, the "expectation of some contingent future about to follow on our action" (*Emotions and Will*, p. 525).

Given Bain's analysis of the way feeling and belief affect volition, we might expect his conception of the act of persuasion to involve two processes: creating the sensation of pleasure or pain in another person and instilling belief that the recommended action will sustain or alleviate it. In his *Rhetoric*, when Bain describes the first of three types of persuasion through the feelings—persuasion based on the audience's own pleasures and pains—he raises just these issues:

> To awaken us to act for our future pleasures, these must be described in adequate language, and with circumstances of credibility. If the pleasures and pains have been already experienced, we should need only to be reminded of them. . . . Feelings that have not been experienced must be described by combining those that have; attachment to an inanimate

thing, as a house, or a garden, or a locality, may be pictured by reference to affection for a person. . . .

To induce the belief that from a certain course of action future pleasures or pains will ensue, it is requisite to appeal to something parallel in the experience of those addressed, or to fire the imagination by means of lively descriptions. (pp. 201–02)

Thus by the associative workings of the mind, the feelings that precede volition and the necessary belief in the recommended action can both be made real to the audience.

The second type of emotional appeal that Bain describes— the appeal to an audience's sympathy—is based on an Aristotelian principle reshaped by Bain's psychology of volition. Aristotle defines pity as "a sense of pain at what we take to be . . . an evil of a destructive or painful kind, which befalls one who does not deserve it, which we think we ourselves or some one allied to us might likewise suffer. . . ."[10] For Bain too, pity is itself a source of pain and is therefore directly connected with volition. "The mere idea of pain is apt to be painful," he writes in *The Emotions and the Will*, "as when I see another person in distress; the more thoroughly we are possessed with that idea, the more are we afflicted or depressed by it" (p. 532). In the *Rhetoric*, Bain converts this notion into a technique of persuasion. "When we enter into the pain of another person," he writes, "we are prompted to work for the alleviation of that pain, as if we ourselves were the sufferers. . . . To rouse sympathy, or call into exercise the disinterested impulses [of the audience], an orator presents a strong and intelligible case of distress, misery, or sorrow" (p. 204). The idea is Aristotle's, but it is enlarged by Bain's theory of pleasure and pain and their link with willed action.

In the third section of his chapter on persuasion through the feelings, which analyzes the role of direct appeals to the whole range of an audience's emotions, Bain asserts that any emotion, not just pity or sympathy, can influence the will. Bain's comments on the psychological effect of the emotions on perception and judgment are strikingly similar to Aristotle's observation that the "same thing does not appear the same to men when they are friendly and when they hate, nor when they are angry and when they are in gentle mood; in these different moods the same thing will appear either wholly different in kind, or different as to magnitude" (*The Rhetoric of Aristotle*, p. 91). In *The Emotions and the Will*, Bain notes that "these various emotions, while they do not alter the facts themselves, alter the mode of looking at them; determining the mind to dwell upon one class of appearances, and to overlook another class as completely as if those did not exist." Again, though, Bain goes beyond the observed phenomenon to explain it in terms of association psychology:

> The careful examination of these phenomena leads to no other conclusion than this, that, when a feeling strongly occupies the mind, the objects in harmony with it are maintained in the view, and all others repelled and ignored. There is a fight between an emotional excitement and the natural course of the intellectual associations. . . . Emotion tampers with the intellectual trains, as a culprit would fain do with the witnesses in his case, keeping out of the way all that are adverse to the interest of the moment. (pp. 545–46)

In his *Rhetoric*, Bain draws on this principle to explain how an orator may use emotional appeals to distort the audience's perceptions. He contends that the emotions operate not only as pleasures or pains that trigger human volition according to fixed laws of association but also as forces that may confuse or block those associations. Used as inflammatory forces, the emotions subvert the natural processes of volition, "disturbing the fair calculations of the will, and inducing us to act without reference to our pleasures or our pains." For example, fear may act as "a tremulous and unhinging excitement, under which the powers are enfeebled, and rational calculation interfered with; every other interest being sacrificed to the morbid impulse" (p. 205). Bain ignores the ethical question involved in evoking emotions for the purpose of "unhinging" the rationality of one's audience and focuses instead on the way a skillful orator can apply the psychological laws that govern volition.

Apart from Bain's theories on the natural origin of figures of speech in the mind's operations, his applications of psychology to rhetoric indicate that he was primarily interested in the mind of the reader rather than that of the writer, that is, in the way psychology can account for and predict the effects that rhetoric may achieve. This emphasis aligns him more closely with the tradition of eighteenth-century rhetoric than with the direction of modern composition research, which has begun to investigate the way in which psychology can explain how discourse is produced. In modern research, as Loren S. Barritt and Barry M. Kroll observe, "the cognitive-developmental approach shifts the emphasis from the *what* of composing (the product) to the *how* of composing (the process). The theory leads one to ask how a composing skill develops and how a person is able to accomplish certain cognitive tasks."[11]

But we should not conclude that Bain's attempt to offer a sophisticated psychological underpinning for at least some rhetorical principles has only antiquarian interest. Rather, his accomplishments are important because they belong to the rhetorical tradition that provides a framework for evaluating modern research. "We cannot understand what is happening," writes Richard Young on the history of rhetorical invention in a recent essay, "unless we understand what happened. Furthermore, without a knowledge of history, we have no way of knowing what is genuinely new, what is redundant, what is promising, what has been tried before and found wanting."[12] If Bain's theories strike us today as incomplete or inadequate, they should in doing so make us more sensitive to change in our discipline and suspicious of the principles we rely on now in our attempts to understand and teach rhetoric. Bain's work is important not because it offers immutable truths but because it prompts us to look ever further into our discipline for better answers and, indeed, more complicated questions.[13]

Notes

[1] Some important recent essays describing alternative approaches to the paragraph are conveniently collected in *Rhetoric and Composition: A Sourcebook for Teachers*, ed. Richard L. Graves (Rochelle Park, N.J.: Hayden, 1976), pp. 151–211.

[2] For two discussions of Bain's contribution to paragraph theory, see Paul C. Rodgers, Jr., "Alexander Bain and the Rise of the Organic Paragraph," *Quarterly Journal of Speech*, 51 (1965), 399–408, and Ned A. Shearer, "Alexander Bain and the Genesis of Paragraph Theory," *Quarterly Journal of Speech*, 58 (1972), 408–17.

[3] Edwin Herbert Lewis, *The History of the English Paragraph* (1894; facsim. rpt. New York: AMS, 1970), p. 29.

[4] Alexander Bain, *Autobiography* (London: Longmans, 1904), p. 49.

[5] Daniel N. Robinson, ed., *The Emotions and the Will*, by Alexander Bain, Significant Contributions to the History of Psychology 1750–1920, Series A: Orientations, Vol. v (Washington, D.C.: Univ. Publications of America, 1977), p. xxxvii.

[6] Bain, *Autobiography*, pp. 277–88. Bain published the second edition of *The Senses and the Intellect* in February 1864 and began his *Rhetoric* two months later. During 1865, when the *Rhetoric* was taking shape, he was also at work on the second edition of *The Emotions and the Will*, which appeared in November 1865. Bain's *Rhetoric* was published in March 1866, and the third edition of *The Senses and the Intellect* followed in 1868. Citations to these three works in the text are to the first edition of *English Composition and Rhetoric: A Manual* (London: Longmans, 1866), the second edition of *The Emotions and the Will* (London: Long-

mans, 1865), and the third edition of *The Senses and the Intellect* (London: Longmans, 1868).

[7] A short discussion of Bain's grouping of figures of speech may also be found in Ned A. Shearer, "Psychology as Foundation to Rhetoric: Alexander Bain and Association Psychology's Relation to Rhetorical Theory," *Western Speech*, 35 (1971), 165–66.

[8] Albert Raymond Kitzhaber, "Rhetoric in American Colleges 1850–1900," Diss. Univ. of Washington 1953, p. 278.

[9] Frank J. D'Angelo, *A Conceptual Theory of Rhetoric* (Cambridge, Mass.: Winthrop, 1975), p. 16.

[10] *The Rhetoric of Aristotle*, trans. Lane Cooper (Englewood Cliffs, N.J.: Prentice-Hall, 1932), p. 120.

[11] Loren S. Barritt and Barry M. Kroll, "Some Implications of Cognitive-Developmental Psychology for Research in Composing," in *Research on Composing: Points of Departure*, ed. Charles R. Cooper and Lee Odell (Urbana: National Council of Teachers of English, 1978), pp. 50–51.

[12] Richard Young, "Invention: A Topographical Survey," in *Teaching Composition: Ten Bibliographical Essays*, ed. Gary Tate (Fort Worth: Texas Christian Univ. Press, 1976), p. 3.

[13] Research for this article was begun during the 1979 National Endowment for the Humanities Summer Seminar conducted by Richard Young at Carnegie-Mellon University. The author is grateful to the NEH for providing this support.

10

Three Nineteenth- Century Rhetoricians: The Humanist Alternative to Rhetoric as Skills Management

NAN JOHNSON

Humanist approaches to rhetorical theory have traditionally defined rhetorical interaction as a socially relevant activity involving a speaker and an audience who share certain interests. Throughout the history of rhetoric as an educational discipline, rhetoricians interested in human nature and human affairs have considered self-expression, communication, and the relation between language and culture to be rhetoric's most significant concerns. The concept of rhetorical discourse as a communicative force is the foundation of Greco-Roman rhetorical theory, and texts faithful to classical models discuss rhetoric as a language activity that shapes belief, behavior, and values.[1] Such approaches stress that as a relational activity rhetoric must take into account sociological influences on human response. This tradition persists in modern rhetorical theory in the work of theorists like Kenneth Burke, Wayne Booth, and Richard Weaver, who have reintroduced to modern rhetoric the view that rhetorical discourse is essentially communicative in substance and socially responsible in its aims.[2]

Although a humanistic perspective on rhetoric and education has enjoyed remarkable longevity in the rhetorical tradition as a whole, this approach has been opposed in every historical period by educators who insist that rhetorical education should focus on the teaching of specialized skills.[3] In the early nineteenth century this emphasis on craft dominated instruction in rhetoric; rhetoric was taught primarily as the skill of argument, arrangement, and stylistic ornamentation. The innovative textbooks of Franz Theremin, Henry

105

Day, and Matthew Hope reacted against this exclusive emphasis on organization and style and attempted to restore a traditional humanistic orientation to the pedagogical practice of the period.[4]

Before the publication of Theremin's *Eloquence a Virtue* (1844), Day's *Elements of the Art of Rhetoric* (1850), and Hope's *Princeton Textbook in Rhetoric* (1854), rhetorical education in American colleges was generally dominated by the extremely popular English rhetorics of Hugh Blair, George Campbell, and Richard Whately.[5] Blair's *Lectures on Rhetoric and Belles Lettres* (1783) and Whately's *Elements of Rhetoric* (1828) were used most frequently. In *Philosophy of Rhetoric* (1778), Campbell was preoccupied with a highly complex discussion of the relation between rhetoric and associationist psychology; this preoccupation limited the usefulness of his work as a classroom text. Whately's *Elements*, devoted entirely to the study of argumentation, emphasized arrangement to the exclusion of invention, while Blair's *Lectures* focused on techniques of style and delivery and relied substantially on the goal of the belles lettres curriculum to cultivate taste and elegance in language usage and literary criticism.[6] In the 1820s, the rhetorical education of the average college student consisted mainly of studying Blair, Campbell, and Whately in some combination between the freshman and senior years. This course of study relied on the memorization of stylistic rules and argumentative structures as a basis for composing formal essays on literary works and abstract persuasive topics. Day, Hope, and William Shedd (who translated Theremin's work *Eloquence a Virtue* from the German) intended their textbooks to provide a badly needed alternative to this standard rhetorical curriculum.

Theremin's work was originally published in 1814 in Berlin. Shedd remarks in the preface to his 1844 translation that Theremin's philosophically based rhetoric served as a necessary correction to the widespread view that rhetoric was "a mere collection of rules respecting the structure of sentences and the garnish of expression."[7] That Shedd's translation of *Eloquence a Virtue* went through ten editions between 1844 and 1897 is evidence that he was not alone in his belief that a humanistic perspective should be added to curriculum offerings. Theremin's rhetoric stressed that the central function of discourse was to "convey an idea of truth to an audience." Shedd believed that this communicative view of rhetoric enabled the student to discover a personal sense of truth and the means to express it. He remarks:

> a student is headed right by it and is taught to apply his best power to the evolution of truth and the production of

thought in his own mind ... the expression of thought becomes a sincere process and the mind, while giving utterance to its reflections, is really contributing to the moral culture and development of the ... man. (p. iii)

In introducing his intention in *Eloquence a Virtue*, Theremin observes:

It has often surprised me that while in modern times the theory of Fine Arts and especially of Poetry, has reached so high a degree of clearness and completeness, Rhetoric still consists of unconnected principles ... and is not competent to guide the practice of Eloquence by sure rules or to give satisfactory information with respect to the nature and qualities of the subject it treats. (p. 51)

Theremin objects to the absence of philosophical principles in rhetorical theory. He seeks to purify the discipline of the excesses of the elocutionary and belles lettres movements by demonstrating that rhetoric is not a knack or a style but rather a fundamental human power founded on basic impulses. Three concepts underlie Theremin's theory of rhetorical discourse: (1) that persuasion is a communicative act essential to harmonious living, (2) that audience identification and assent to commonly shared values is the most effective and moral basis for persuasion, and (3) that a consideration of values on the part of the speaker will generate both thought and appealing subject matter.

Theremin contends that all motivation and truth, and hence all persuasion, stem from the pursuit of the ethical ideals of duty, virtue, and happiness. He defines rhetoric as "that action, that force that develops this universal ethical impulse." Rhetoric acts to change beliefs and actions according to the ethical ideals Theremin cites; therefore, persuasion relies on the speaker's ability to show how the ethical idea central to the argument will allow the audience to pursue these ideals. Theremin insists that the ethical impulse is the motive ground for all behavior.

Ethical ideas are destined to be embodied in life, they lie in the reason, and must be presupposed to be in every man considered as being endowed with reason, and are, moreover actually indwelling in everyone. (p. 74)

The plan of the speech depends on what ethical idea the speaker believes he or she should emphasize to respond to the ethical impulses of a particular audience. Theremin argues that the speaker should depend not on a formulaic plan that will generate argumentative structure but on personal knowledge of the particular situation and the demands for truth of those involved.

> The counter-action which the orator expects from the hearer determines him to begin now with this Idea and now with that . . . and hence no universal rule can be laid down regarding a Plan of this sort since existing circumstances and relations have so great an influence upon it. (p. 120)

The invention of argumentative discourse is dependent upon what Theremin calls the dialogical quality of rhetoric. The rhetorician must be committed to the principle of discovering shared truths, truths that will in turn generate the most effective means of expression and fulfill his or her purpose. Theremin describes the rhetorical dialogue as an "attempt to transfer something that has been generated in the depths of the soul, into another person, which can be done only in proportion as the orator himself possess that which is to be produced" (p. 152). Through this kind of dialogue, this sharing of significant truths, thought becomes the "sincere process" that Shedd emphasizes as the important aspect of Theremin's theory and insists should be added to "that which the liberally educated student should know" (p. x).

The significance of Theremin's notion of audience orientation is twofold: his view that discourse influences minds to moral action is startlingly like the views of the New Rhetoric that stress the interactional and social significance of discourse, and Shedd's translation of *Eloquence a Virtue* marks the first appearance in American rhetorical theory of a rhetoric that is humanistically based. As such, *Eloquence a Virtue* can rightfully be considered the first innovation in American rhetorical education.

Theremin intended to rescue rhetorical practice from overspecialization, from becoming merely a sum of its systemized parts. In *Elements of the Art of Rhetoric*, first published in 1850, Henry Day contributes to the same effort by reaffirming the communicative function of rhetorical discourse and restoring invention to rhetorical education by presenting it as a primary division of rhetorical activity.[8] Invention was not treated by the texts of the day, and Day objected that "the attention of learners has thus been turned chiefly or solely upon style" (p. iv). Day describes what he considers the result of this excessive attention to style and the solution to the problem it creates.

> The consequence has been, as might naturally be expected where *manner* is the chief object of regard, that exercises in

composition have been exceedingly repulsive and profitless drudgeries. . . . On the other hand, . . . if the mind be turned mainly on the *matter* the thought to be presented and the design of presenting it, the exercise of composition becomes a most interesting, attractive and profitable exercise. (p. iv)

Day intended his classically flavored treatment of invention to make rhetoric the "positively invigorating and developing art" that it was in earlier periods when no one aspect of the rhetorical process was emphasized to the detriment of others (p. iv).

Theremin objects to the limitations of a rhetorical discipline practiced without a philosophical commitment; Day argues with what he considers the extremely narrow definition of rhetoric in the popular texts of the period, specifically in Whately's *Elements of Rhetoric* and Blair's *Lectures on Rhetoric and Belles Lettres*. While Day insists that rhetoric is not properly a part of the study of poetry and literature, Blair emphasizes their study by defining the object of rhetorical education as the instruction of how to speak and write with purity, grace, and taste (pp. 1–12). Day argues that defining rhetoric as stylistic ornamentation completely ignores the interpersonal nature of discourse. Richard Whately deals exclusively with rhetoric as the skill of argumentation and arrangement and in so doing, Day points out in his preface, fails to take into account all the purposes for which rhetorical skill is needed. Day bases his text on the following inclusive definition:

> the art of rhetoric proposes to explain the principles by which we discourse or communicate thought and feeling to other minds, and to furnish the means of acquiring a skill and dexterity in the use of this power. (p. 2)

Explicit in this definition of rhetoric is an emphasis on self-expression, communication, and the affective force of skillful discourse. This view is conspicuously absent from the texts of the early nineteenth century. Communicative discourse, Day argues, has important functions in everyday life, and rhetorical education should address those interactional and functional purposes. One of the most significant contributions that Day made to American rhetorical practice was to extend the province of rhetoric to include explanatory or informative discourse. Informative discourse is such a major part of our contemporary pedagogical concerns that it is difficult to imagine a time when educators had to be persuaded to include expository writing in writing classes. Day urged this inclusion, and his text introduced what has subsequently become a common feature of our writing curricula.

In addition to outlining the inventional procedures for persuasion, Day defines the inventional processes he believes are appropriate for the development of explanatory essays: narration,
description, analysis, exemplification, and comparison and contrast.[9]
Our modern composition texts commonly feature these processes as
modes of paragraph development and essay organization. Their presentation in contemporary texts is critically different from the way
Day intended these processes to be used. Day discusses narration,
description, exemplification, and so on in terms of the kinds of ideas
these approaches to composing generate and how such ideas affect
what he calls "human understanding" or audience response. The
heuristic and affective potential of these inventional processes has
received little pedagogical attention in twentieth-century texts,
which commonly feature these processes as abstract organizational
forms.[10]

Day's efforts to refocus pedagogical attention on the importance of communicative purpose and the central activity of invention
in composing were nearly revolutionary in his time; his text, extremely popular and highly imitated, went through eleven editions
between 1850 and 1889. Because textbook authors in the nineteenth
century commonly absorbed whole tracts by other authors without
acknowledgment, it is difficult to trace explicitly the line of Day's influence, but, we need only look at the general presence of explanatory writing and the four modes of paragraph development in the
texts that follow his and in contemporary texts to see the extent to
which Day's ideas were incorporated into standard classroom pedagogy. Like Theremin, Day defined rhetoric as a culturally significant
and forceful faculty and opposed instruction that was based on a system of stylistic rules and procedures. His intention to establish a
communicative paradigm for rhetorical education echos in the efforts of similarly committed contemporary rhetoricians, like Richard
Young, James Kinneavy, and W. Ross Winterowd, who emphasize
the theoretical and pedagogical significance of expressive purpose
and inventional heuristics in learning to compose.[11]

Matthew Hope's *Princeton Textbook in Rhetoric*, first published in 1854, was strongly influenced by the communicative point of
view articulated by Day and Theremin.[12] Hope borrowed heavily
from each and comments in his preface that "suggestive assistance"
from their texts shaped a great portion of his own textbook. The
Princeton Textbook did not make any one original contribution to
pedagogical theory but preserved and thereby encouraged the communicative principles of Theremin and Day. Hope imitates Day's inventional focus and Theremin's definition of persuasion as an ethical

and socially responsible art. Hope bases his text on this definition of rhetoric:

> The rhetorical process involves not only the inception of power in the human spirit but the control in the required direction, and with the required degree of force to accomplish a given end. (p. 3)

On the basis of this definition, Hope advocates a pedagogy that presents rhetoric as a self-expressive and socially responsible communication skill that recognizes the importance language plays in our everyday lives. The *Princeton Textbook* emphasizes a persuasive skill that deals with matters of personal and cultural truth. Hope recommends that this text replace Whately's and be read in conjunction with Day's *Elements of Rhetoric* and Theremin's *Eloquence a Virtue*. Obviously, he intended to completely replace the Whately-Blair curriculum with a more functional emphasis on discourse as a means of self-discovery and social interaction.

Hope is quick to disavow any relation between rhetoric and belles lettres, saying that "literature and poetry are not within the proper sphere of rhetoric." A central focus on style could not help the students to grasp how writing could serve their individual and varied needs. Echoing Day's criticism of Whately's text, Hope objects to Whately's narrow definition of rhetoric as persuasion and criticizes Whately for not addressing what Hope calls "the practical ends of students preparing for professional life" (p. iv). Hope's belief that students should acquire a generally effective discourse skill reflects the sentiments of Day and Theremin and contrasts sharply with the views espoused by the stylistic and systematic rhetorics of the time.

In resisting the overspecialization of pedagogical practice in the nineteenth century, Hope, Theremin, and Day became participants in an age-old disagreement about the role rhetoric should play in education. Our contemporary discipline is similarly divided: Should rhetorical education focus on teaching the skills of writing or should it address discourse competence as a personally expressive and socially significant force? Are these pedagogical directions necessarily exclusive? The overall goals of contemporary humanist approaches to the teaching of writing appear to be at odds with the aims of the "back-to-basic skills" curriculum for composition. In a recent article entitled "Literature and Literacy," published in the Modern Language Association's *Profession 79*, Joseph Duffey, then chairman of the National Endowment for the Humanities, urges teachers of writing to direct their energies toward instilling in students an awareness of the vital connection among language skill, self-expression, and societal contribution. Duffey remarks:

> It is possible to teach literacy, in the narrowest and most technical way, simply as the development of skills. But it is also possible to recognize that student voices are a part of a culture and that mastery of language skills is a way of actively participating in that culture. In that sense, the teaching of language skills is a ... process of building society just as surely as the study of literature helps to build a tradition.[13]

Duffey objects to teaching writing only as the mastery of skills. His concern that students need to be made aware that each has an individual writing voice and that language competence can have both social impact and cultural relevance is reminiscent of Shedd's insistence that a humanistic approach to teaching was needed to encourage the student to "apply his best power to the evolution of truth. . . ." In asking the English profession to restore traditionally humanistic principles to writing pedagogy, Duffey takes issue with the assumed adequacy of skills-oriented writing classes.

Many educators might question whether teachers of writing can rightfully involve themselves in the complex task of raising students' consciousness of the relation of language, culture, and self-expression when those same students are confused about grammar, punctuation, organization, topic sentences, the difference between specific and general, and just about everything else having to do with prose composition. Because our young people's literacy skills have declined dramatically, many teachers have rededicated themselves to the belief that a greater emphasis on grammar and formal organizational structures is needed in composition curricula. Those who adhere to the back-to-basics approach to language instruction assume that students cannot write effectively or even competently because they have never been taught basic information about how to write correctly and that if these students are exposed to standards of correctness, or what E. D. Hirsch has recently termed "typical rules and maxims," the know-how will subsequently evolve.[14] Hirsch's *The Philosophy of Composition* (1977) is the most recent and widely popularized argument in favor of the skills-oriented approach to composition. Stressing the importance of dealing practically with the "present crisis in literacy," Hirsch observes that "humanistic" goals in composition teaching are inappropriate. The proper province of composition, he argues, is the instruction of form: "learning how to write . . . assumes the separation of linguistic form and content" (p.

141). Logic, literature, and rhetoric have no bearing on the teaching of highly specific elements of craft. And to believe otherwise falsely assumes that composition comes "under some humanistic subject matter. . . ."

> To learn to write is to gain practical, not theoretical knowledge. Writing needs to be taught as a practical, not a theoretical, subject. The teacher of drawing asks his students to make drawings, and then comments on what his students have produced. That is the basic character of teaching in all the practical arts including the art of writing. (p. 143)

Hirsch's characterization of writing instruction as "practical" in its intention and method typifies the frame of mind of those who support a skills-oriented writing curriculum. Such an orientation emphasizes the practice of specific skills of composition and the memorization of features of grammar. James Britton, Janet Emig, and Donald Murray have argued against such pedagogical methods and were among the first composition theorists to attempt to direct pedagogical practice away from an exclusive emphasis on the technical skills of craft and toward a presentation of writing as a communicative process.[15] The process approach to pedagogy assumes that students should be encouraged to view language competence as a self-expressive and socially relevant activity and not solely as the mastery of grammatical rules and formal structural schema. This approach to writing instruction recognizes "that student voices are a part of a culture" (Duffey, p. 175).

This outline of the conflicting aims of the back-to-basics curriculum and the process pedagogy is intended to suggest, rather than inclusively document, the substance of current controversies over appropriate teaching responsibilities and methods. This disagreement is widespread but not entirely without remedy if we assume that teachers are not necessarily faced with an either/or choice. By combining a skills orientation with a humanist definition of the aims of discourse, teachers can provide students with information about what writing is and can encourage an understanding of what writing can do. Theremin, Day, and Hope reformulated pedagogical priorities by incorporating the specific skills of style and argumentative arrangement within larger outlines of techniques for generating and shaping self-expressive and communicative prose. In *Errors and Expectations* (1977), Mina Shaughnessy advocates a pedagogical approach that retains a balance between a humanistic perspective on language competence and an emphasis on the importance of skills and standards.[16] Shaughnessy argues that the rules of correctness ("typical rules and maxims") should be presented to students as significant, replicable standards because of the way these standards facilitate the communicative intentions of writers.

Although speakers and listeners, writers and readers, are in one sense engaged in a cooperative effort to understand one another, they are also in conflict over the amount of effort each will expend on the other. That is, the speaker or writer wants to say what he has to say with as little energy as possible and the listener or reader wants to understand with as little energy as possible. Errors, however, are unintentional and unprofitable intrusions on the consciousness of the reader. They demand energy without giving any return in meaning; they shift the reader's attention from where he is going (meaning) to how he is getting there (code). (p. 12)

Shaughnessy's communicative perspective illustrates that, if we remember that craft is a means to an end, not an end in itself, we can close the gap between the "practical" aims of our contemporary skills pedagogy and the humanistic goals of teaching writing as a "part of culture." Shedd, Day, and Hope found that the overemphasis on "manner" so prevalent in rhetorical education in the middle nineteenth century failed to respond to the student's need to understand why writing well should be personally or socially valuable. It is far more expedient to instruct students in what is grammatically correct than it is to explain to them that there are reasons why certain normative ideas about correctness and coherence have evolved. It is less frustrating, and bureaucratically far more attractive, to concentrate on the development of lab modules on the comma, the compound sentence, and the thesis statement than to discuss the same constituents of "good" writing as rhetorical cues that facilitate the ability to discover thought and share it with others.

The challenge of this more difficult task confronted humanistic rhetoricians of the nineteenth century. This challenge now confronts those members of our profession who believe that rhetorical education should aspire to more than the caretaking of maintenance literacy.

Notes

[1] Classical rhetoricians in general assumed that the skill of oratory was communicative in purpose. In the oral culture of Greece and Rome, persuasive speaking necessarily entailed an awareness of specific audience interests and social, political, and judicial issues. The art of rhetoric was consubstantial with achieved effects. Classically based texts, such as Au-

gustine's *On Christian Doctrine* (396) and Thomas Wilson's *Art of Rhetoric* (1553), retained the emphasis on relevant, communicative intention that was a basic principle in classical works such as Plato's *Gorgias*, Aristotle's *Rhetoric*, Cicero's *De Oratore*, and Quintilian's *Institutio Oratoria*.

2 Burke, Booth, and Weaver agree that the aim of rhetoric is to induce agreement and assent by presenting motives and values with which an audience will identify. These rhetoricians argue that rhetoric does not merely guide us on how to arrange language and ideas but comprises a theory of communication. For more on this approach to modern rhetoric, see Kenneth Burke, *A Rhetoric of Motives* (Berkeley: Univ. of California Press, 1969); Wayne Booth, *Modern Dogma and the Rhetoric of Assent* (Chicago: Univ. of Chicago Press, 1974); and Richard Weaver, "Language Is Sermonic," in *Dimensions of Rhetorical Scholarship*, ed. Roger E. Nebergall (Norman: Univ. of Oklahoma Press, 1963), pp. 49–63.

3 Rhetorical education has often been divided between instruction in highly technical, aesthetically oriented skills and instruction in arts of persuasive communication. In the Middle Ages, rhetorical education included instruction in *ars praedicandi*, the art of preaching; *ars dictaminis*, the highly technical craft of letter writing; and *ars poetica*, the skill of stylistic application of figures and tropes to poetry. In the Renaissance, classical treatments of rhetoric such as Wilson's *Art of Rhetoric* (1553) and Erasmus' *De Copia* (1512) competed with Peter Ramus' *Dialectic* (1556), which challenged the integrity of rhetoric as a humanist discipline by proposing that invention and arrangement be reallocated to the province of logic. In Ramist hands, rhetoric became the skill of ornament. Similarly, the belletristic rhetorics of the late eighteenth and early nineteenth centuries and the elocutionary emphasis prevalent in rhetorics of the same period presented rhetoric as a mastery of the technique of style and delivery. See Thomas Sheridan's influencial elocutionist treatise, *Lectures on Elocution* (1762).

4 Warren Guthrie considers William Shedd's translation of Theremin and the textbooks of Day and Hope to have contributed to "asserting the functional significance of rhetoric" in the middle nineteenth century. He summarizes their works in "The Development of Rhetorical Theory in America," *Speech Monographs*, 16, No. 1 (1949), 106–13.

5 Hugh Blair, *Lectures on Rhetoric and Belles Lettres*, ed. Harold F. Harding (Carbondale: Southern Illinois Univ. Press, 1965); George Campbell, *The Philosophy of Rhetoric*, ed. Lloyd F. Bitzer (Carbondale: Southern Illinois Univ. Press, 1963); and Richard Whately, *Elements of Rhetoric*, ed. Douglas Ehninger (Carbondale: Southern Illinois Univ. Press, 1963).

6 For information on the circulation of these texts see Warren Guthrie, "The Development of Rhetorical Theory in America," *Speech Monographs*, 15, No. 1, (1948), 61–70.

7 Franz Theremin, *Eloquence a Virtue: An Outline of a Systematic Rhetoric*, trans. William T. Shedd, (Philadelphia: Smith, English and Co., 1859), p. 1. When Shedd translated Theremin's text in 1844, he was a professor

of liberal arts at Vermont College. The appearance of Shedd's edition strongly influenced Day's *Elements* and provided the basis for Hope's reorganization of the aims of argument in *The Princeton Textbook.* Shedd's preface to Theremin's text is a lengthy defense of the ethical perspective and a critique of the limited scope of the rhetorics of the time, pp. 1–50. Theremin's treatise itself is organized in two books, Book I on invention and Book II on elocution. Under invention, Theremin defines the philosophical aims of rhetoric and specifies how subject matter, arrangement, and the character of the orator relate to the ethical motives of the audience. Book II discusses pathetic appeal and style under elocution. Theremin treats style only in terms of effects and the quality of achieving vivacity. Unfortunately, there are no modern editions of Shedd's translation. Former editions can be obtained from university libraries including Brown University, Harvard, and Rutgers.

8 Henry N. Day, *Elements of the Art of Rhetoric* (New York: A. S. Barnes and Burn, 1866), p. iii. Other references to Day are to this edition and will be cited parenthetically. Day observes in his preface that "valuable suggestions" were "derived from diverse German writers as . . . Theremin." Day's text incorporates Theremin's ethical and communicative perspective on persuasion. *Elements of the Art of Rhetoric* is organized in two parts under the headings "Invention" and "Style" (exactly Theremin's divisions). Under "Invention," Day discusses the "parts of invention," persuasion, and explanatory discourse. Day defines narration, description, analysis, excitation, and comparison and contrast as inventional processes for explanatory discourse. Under the "Style," Day discusses the "absolute properties" of language, euphony, harmony, rhythm, and melody; the "subjective properties" of language, significance, continuousness, and naturalness; and the "objective properties" of language, clearness, energy, and elegance.

9 Day's definition of the kinds of explanatory discourse and his view that explanatory discourse is a kind of rhetorical activity predate Alexander Bain's similar treatment in *English Composition and Rhetoric* (1867) in which Bain defines narration and description as modes of discourse.

10 Notable exceptions are James L. Kinneavy, *A Theory of Discourse* (Englewood Cliffs, N.J.: Prentice-Hall, 1971). On pp. 35–37, Kinneavy treats narration, description, and so on in terms of how each mode corresponds to the principles of thought. See also W. Ross Winterowd, *Contemporary Writer* (New York: Harcourt, 1975), pp. 28–109, and Janice M. Lauer, Gene Montague, Andrea Lunsford, Janet Emig, *Four Worlds of Writing* (New York: Harper, 1980).

11 See Richard E. Young, Alton L. Becker, Kenneth L. Pike, *Phetoric, Discovery and Change* (New York: Harcourt, 1970); Richard Young, "Paradigms and Problems: Needed Research in Rhetorical Invention," in *Research on Composing: Points of Departure*, ed. Charles Cooper and Lee Odel (Urbana: National Council of Teachers of English, 1978), pp. 29–47; and W. Ross Winterowd, "Topics and Levels in the Composing Process," in *Rhetoric and Composition*, ed. Richard L. Graves (Rochelle Park, N.J.: Hayden, 1976), pp. 313–23.

¹² Matthew Boyd Hope, *The Princeton Textbook on Rhetoric* (Princeton: John T. Robinson, 1859), p. 2. All other references to this text will be cited parenthetically. Hope's text was written for "the use of the author's own pupils." The major portion of the text is devoted to a discussion of argument on how to "convey the conviction of truth, in the light of its own evidence to the mind of another party." The text has four sections; Parts I and III deal with kinds of argument and refutation, invention, and "organic" arrangement. Book II of Section III treats style. Section IV deals with elocution and discusses qualities of the voice, matters of delivery and gesture. Hope's treatment of style is influenced by his contention that style is "a living product of the mind, giving dynamic expression to thought, with the view of producing an effect on other minds" (p. 169).

¹³ Joseph Duffey, "Literature and Literacy," *Profession 79* (New York: MLA, 1979), p. 19. For a similar discussion of the importance of a humanist approach to the teaching of composition see John Warnock, "New Rhetoric and the Grammar of Pedagogy," *Freshman English News*, 5 (1976). Warnock observes that "to say that we must find ways to make our students aware of themselves as creators of their culture, and not just servants of it, is to take both a political and a rhetorical stance. This makes of rhetoric a high calling indeed" (p. 21).

¹⁴ E. D. Hirsch, Jr., *The Philosophy of Composition* (Chicago: Univ. of Chicago Press, 1977), p. 144. Other references are cited parenthetically. Hirsch proposes that teachers of composition can best teach writing by teaching students "readability," a quality of style that emphasizes "speed of closure and semantic adequacy." Hirsch equates "readability" with "communicative writing."

¹⁵ See Janet Emig, "The Composing Process of Twelfth Graders," National Council of Teachers of English Research Report No. 13 (Urbana: National Council of Teachers of English, 1971); Donald M. Murray, "Teach Writing as a Process Not Product," in *Rhetoric and Composition*, ed. Richard L. Graves (Rochelle Park, N.J.: Hayden, 1976), pp. 79–82; James Birton et al., *Development of Writing Abilities 11–18* (London: Macmillan Education, 1975); and James Britton, "The Composing Process and the Functions of Writing," in *Research on Composing: Points of Departure*, ed. Charles Cooper and Lee Odel (Urbana: National Council of Teachers of English, 1978), pp. 29–47.

¹⁶ Mina P. Shaughnessy, *Errors and Expectations: A Guide for the Teacher of Basic Writing* (New York: Oxford Univ. Press, 1977). Other references are cited parenthetically. Shaughnessy argues that programs are not the answers to students' learning problems but that teachers can be. Teachers must develop programs in response to the needs of individual student populations. The text proposes a treatment of error that relies on the assumption that if students understand why they are being asked to learn something, they will be disposed to learn it.

11

Two Model Teachers and the Harvardization of English Departments

DONALD C. STEWART

In some ways professions are like people. They are born at certain times in certain circumstances; they go through frequently painful adolescences in which they try to define themselves both for their own sakes and as a way to establish their legitimacy before the general public; and they make choices that significantly affect their entire lives. Once established in their maturity, they put the difficulties and doubts of earlier years behind them and settle into a long period of stability and productivity. Any profession's life span is a capricious thing, however, because it depends on luck, good health, and the length of time that particular profession can serve usefully.

There are important ways, however, in which professions are not like people. Their life spans are often greater, and, most important, the options that confront them in adolescence may appear again in old age, sometimes offering opportunities for renewed vigor and a return to youth.

Now, how old should a profession be before it begins to examine its history—specifically, its reason for coming into being, its philosophy, and its heroes? There is no absolute answer to such a question. Perhaps the best answer is that it should begin to examine itself when it finds its methods, its priorities, and its practitioners out of adjustment with the society that it wishes to serve. Despite recent encouraging changes in some attitudes, I still believe that the profession of English, as practiced by a number of American college and university teachers, is out of adjustment with modern American society and that nothing would be healthier for it now than a searching examination of its reasons for coming into being, its philosophy, and its heroes. Such an examination will lead inevitably to a reassessment of this profession's history, priorities, and practitioners in ways that will be disturbing to many, but recommendations for healthful change are often like bad-tasting medicine or exercise prescribed for flabby muscles. One will be distasteful and the other will hurt, but the benefits obtained from both will more than compensate for the discomforts.

My examination of our profession's history is far from comprehensive. It focuses only on the careers of two men: Francis James Child and Fred Newton Scott. A large segment of our profession has venerated the one and forgotten the other. That mistake, I believe, is deeply symptomatic of what has been wrong with our profession for many decades.

In the late nineteenth century the young profession of English came to a fork in the road, and with little hesitation, I suspect, made its choice and confidently set out on a path with which it was and has been fully comfortable. I say "young" profession somewhat arbitrarily, recognizing that it is difficult to say that at any particular date the modern profession of English was born but willing to argue that what we today call "the profession" began in the last quarter of the nineteenth century.[1] I choose 1876 as pivotal because in that year Johns Hopkins, the first American university to imitate the German universities in methods and goals (offering elective courses and training research scholars), offered a chair in English literature to Francis Child, Harvard's fourth Boylston Professor of Rhetoric. Harvard, unwilling to give up Child, created a similar chair for him and made his assistant, Adams Sherman Hill, the fifth Boylston Professor of Rhetoric.[2]

Child had waited twenty-five years for that kind of appointment, despairing at times of its ever coming, complaining bitterly at others about the years he had wasted correcting freshman themes. He had been the Boylston Professor since 1851, when Edward T. Channing, the third occupant ⸺ ːhe chair, retired. During the thirty-two years Channing served as Boylston Professor, he had effected a number of subtle changes in the nature and scope of his office. The most significant, for my purposes, were two emphases that appeared repeatedly in his work: his interest in the study of literature rather than in the tradition of rhetoric and a profound distrust of oratory as practiced by the ancients.[3] His perception of ancient oratory seems to have been influenced by an imperfect reading of Plato's *Gorgias,* in which the rhetoric of the ancient Sophists is held up to scorn. Channing does not note, however, Plato's differentiation, in the *Gorgias,* between a false and a true rhetoric, and he ignores this distinction as it is more fully worked out in the *Phaedrus,* where Plato defines a noble rhetoric that serves truth and the public welfare.[4]

Channing's literary-critical interests and his conception of

oratory as sophistic were intensified in Francis Child, who was neither by temperament nor by physical appearance an orator. He had
discovered what he really wanted to do between 1849 and 1851 while
studying at Göttingen and Berlin, where he "established a lifetime
devotion to folklore, especially English and Scottish ballads. He fashioned his research habits after Jakob and Wilhelm Grimm, pictures
of whom, it was later reported, he kept on his study wall at Cambridge" (Ried, "Francis Child," p. 272). In 1872 the Danish scholar
and folklorist Svend Grundtvig initiated correspondence with Child,
who thus had the final impetus to push ahead in his scholarly labors.
Grundtvig was particularly useful to Child as a sounding board, helping him work out his scheme for classifying ballads in *The English
and Scottish Popular Ballads*, publication of which began in 1882.[5]
Child finished four volumes of this work; the fifth was completed by
George Lyman Kittredge, Child's most famous pupil.

Although Child served as Boylston Professor from 1851 until
1876, I can find no evidence that he took this job for any reason other
than his desire for a position at Harvard and his trust that time and
Providence would provide something better. Providence, as I have
noted, took its time. A story circulates that on one occasion Child an-
grily kicked a chair across a room, complaining bitterly about the
years he was wasting correcting student themes. He didn't like listening to declamations much better, and he seems not to have performed either task with much imagination. As the years passed, he
increasingly questioned the legitimacy of oratory and composition as
university subjects, because they were too elementary, but one
might point out that he made little effort to raise the level of this
work to that of a true university discipline. As I have already suggested, however, the root of Child's antipathy for rhetoric was his
distrust of it, a distrust inherited from Channing's incomplete understanding of Plato's position on the rhetoric of ancient Greece. Child
never concealed his priorities. He was intent on raising the study of
English literature to the status of a solid academic discipline, and he
was absorbed in his own research. The kind of contact with students
that rhetoric requires could only have irritated him. In fact, Albert
Bushnell Hart wrote that "Francis Child used to say with a disarm-
ing twinkle that the university would never be perfect until we got
rid of all the students."[6]

It would be a mistake, of course, to underestimate the significance of what Child accomplished. In his own work he established
himself as the preeminent literary scholar in America during the last
half of the nineteenth century. Careful study of the Harvard catalog
from 1872 to 1910 shows that he took a struggling elective subject

and turned it into a major discipline. In 1872 Child *was* Harvard's English department, and the battle with the entrenched classical curriculum had just begun in earnest. He taught one course that combined a history of the English language, Shakespearean grammar, and three plays of Shakespeare; another in Anglo-Saxon; and one in English composition and literature. By 1895–96, Child's last year at the university, the department of English listed twenty-six literature courses, among which were surveys; period courses; courses on single figures, such as Shakespeare, Bacon, or Milton; literary criticism; versification; and genre courses. Some were designated primarily for graduates and some were designated as courses for research. Harvard's department had won its battle with the classicists and was moving rapidly toward accomplishing the structure that has characterized most English department programs throughout the twentieth century. Some elective courses in composition were offered, but they were at lower levels and none even faintly suggested that truly advanced work in this field was taking place.

The prestige and influence of the Harvard department, with its increasing emphasis on literary-critical scholarship, significantly helped cause the reduction of rhetoric and composition to second-rate status, despite the numbers of students enrolled in such courses, and the eventual splitting away from English departments of speech and linguistics. Despite some adjustments in the past few years, these still survive. Although the philological and historical emphases that characterized Child's work no longer dominate, English departments for the most part perceive their mission as the study of English and American literature. Composition courses sustain the graduate program; speech and linguistics constitute separate departments. Departmental programs also reflect, from time to time, some popular emphases: studies of film, women's studies, technical writing, and so on. But these studies are superficial and often transitory departures from what English departments perceive their main business to be. It is possible that in a few eccentric places like the University of Southern California, the University of Iowa, and Carnegie-Mellon University, where holders of endowed chairs or department chairs do work in composition, the department's program is more balanced, but even that is not certain. Even with the progress made in recent years, few persons I know would deny that most members of our profession still perceive that their mission is to teach literature and that work in speech, linguistics, and rhetoric is either ancillary or intellectually inferior to work in literature. They find it particularly difficult to conceive of work in rhetoric or composition at an advanced level.

We must turn the clock back again, however, this time to 1889, when Kittredge was in his second year as an instructor in the Harvard department. We know the influence he eventually exerted on the profession. He carried the legacy of Francis Child to its natural fruition. But in 1889 another very different kind of English professor emerged, Fred Newton Scott of Michigan. From the beginning of his professional career, Scott showed a remarkable balance in his academic interests. Although the topic for his doctoral dissertation was "Italian Critics of the Renaissance as a Source for the Earliest English Criticism," his later publications reflect an astonishing variety of competencies. How, for example, can one safely generalize about a bibliography that includes "Boccaccio's *De Genealogia Deorum* and Sidney's *Defense of Poesie*"; *Paragraph Writing* (with Joseph Villiers Denney); *Introduction to the Methods and Materials of Literary Criticism: The Bases in Aesthetics* (with Charles Mills Gayley); *The Teaching of English* (with G. R. Carpenter and F. T. Baker), "The Most Fundamental Differentia of Poetry and Prose"; *Aphorisms for Teachers of English Composition* (with Joseph Villiers Denney); "The Genesis of Speech"; "A Note on Walt Whitman's Prosody"; "Verbal Taboos"; and "The Standard of American Speech"; as well as editions of works by G. H. Lewes, Herbert Spencer, Samuel Johnson, Thomas DeQuincey, and Daniel Webster and translations of the plays of Leonid Andreyeff (with Clarence L. Meader), and the poems of N. A. Nekrasov? There are 105 such titles in the Scott bibliography.[7] In addition, Scott achieved a level of excellence in teaching and service rarely equaled in the history of our profession. In 1933 Louis Strauss, then head of Michigan's English department, said of him:

> Dr. Scott's conception of rhetoric was catholic in the extreme; it was limited only by the range of his own personal interests, which really means that it was not limited at all. Under the spell of his magnetic and stimulating personality his students developed to their utmost capacity. They are to be found everywhere—brilliant teachers, successful writers, and men in every walk of life upon whose tastes and characters his influence is indelibly stamped; and they are not backward in saying so.[8]

Strauss should have said men *and* women, because one thinks immediately of Gertrude Buck, Ruth Weeks, and Helen Mahin, brilliant women who remained loyal to their professor throughout their professional careers.

I cannot, within the limits of this paper, give an adequate

idea of the esteem in which Scott was held by his professional colleagues. One set of facts will have to do. In 1907 he was President of the Modern Language Association; in 1911–13, President of the National Council of Teachers of English; in 1913–14, President of the North Central Association of Colleges and Secondary Schools; and in 1917, President of the American Association of Journalism Teachers. MLA members might be interested to know that Scott was appointed to the nominating committee—which, in effect, chose the association's officers—in 1896, 1900, 1908, 1909, 1910, 1914, and 1915.

Despite the diversity and quality of Scott's literary, pedagogical, and professional activities, however, it was the opinion of his earliest and most brilliant rhetoric Ph.D., Gertrude Buck of Vassar, that Scott's reputation would ultimately rest on his distinctive contributions to rhetorical theory.[9] In general, what were these contributions? Albert Kitzhaber sums them up well:

> Scott . . . made a genuine effort to formulate a comprehensive system of rhetorical theory drawing on new developments in such related disciplines as experimental psychology, linguistics, and sociology. More than this, he tried earnestly to vitalize rhetorical instruction both in the secondary schools and in the colleges; but, though he met with some success for a time in the 1890s, most of his ideas were too new, his recommendations for change too fundamental to be generally accepted. . . . As a scholar, Scott chose not to break with tradition, but rather to find out what the tradition was, where it was going, and what his place in it was. . . . he wanted to retain what was still valid in traditional doctrine, but to use this as a foundation on which to build new theory. His ideas often seemed strikingly unconventional to many people. Students coming to him who had been trained to look at language as primarily a matter of mechanical correctness found that Scott had a more functional view. . . . His keen awareness of the relations of rhetoric to other disciplines, his alertness in keeping abreast of new developments in these disciplines, his view of language as a social phenomenon serving definite human needs, his liberal and informed attitude toward linguistic usage—these, together with his impelling curiosity about literary effects and his conviction that these effects are capable of being studied and described, made graduate work in rhetoric a challenging and rewarding experience. How far his influence extended through the impression that his ideas made on his students it

would be difficult to say. Certain of his students, however, such as Sterling A. Leonard and Ruth M. Weeks, both of whom took master's degrees in rhetoric under Scott, were leaders in the movement that tried to promote a more liberal and scientific view toward language matters in composition courses and textbooks.[10]

No man was more influential than Scott in the reform movement of the nineties, and no man offered more sensible leadership. His recommendations were always thoughtful, always conscious of the larger implications of rhetorical problems. . . . He tried, though unsuccessfully, to secure the adoption of a fuller conception of rhetoric, one that would restore to it the great social importance that it has sometimes had in its long history. Unfortunately, English teachers were not ready then to adopt such a view. Instead, the narrower philosophy of the Harvard group [A. S. Hill, Lebaron Briggs, Barrett Wendell, and their successors] won out, with the result that rhetorical instruction in America until well into the 1930s became, for all practical purposes, little more than instruction in grammar and the mechanics of writing, motivated almost solely by the ideal of superficial correctness.[11]

Kitzhaber's final observation, that the narrower philosophy of the Harvard group won out, is important because that philosophy would never have evolved had it not been for the priorities Francis Child and his disciples established. Once the literature program at Harvard was intact, the rhetoric program steadily decayed intellectually despite sizable enrollments. Furthermore, one may legitimately wonder whether "Harvardization" of English departments in the early part of this century meant that these priorities were carried to other universities.[12]

Where, then, has this brief excursion into the careers of two men, one at Harvard, the other at Michigan, taken us? I have tried to suggest (1) that Francis Child, while raising the study of English literature to the status of a genuine professional discipline, also believed—and perhaps caused those who followed him to believe—that the study of rhetoric or composition was inferior work; (2) that Child valued his scholarly research first and his teaching of literature second and viewed the teaching of composition or rhetoric as at best tolerable, at worst a necessary evil attending an academic position; (3) that Child was the forerunner of a group of Harvard men who accepted his priorities and communicated them to the departments in which they subsequently became powerful; and (4) that these priorities, and not those of Fred Newton Scott—who valued the study of both literature and rhetoric and who maintained an unflagging interest in a tremendous range of language acts, from the most sophisticated belletristic efforts of classic writers to the utterances of children—set the tone in American university English departments and still prevail widely in the late twentieth century.

At the beginning of this paper, I suggested that nearly one hundred years ago, English, as a young profession, embarked on the course that Francis Child had set for it. The result has been the production of numbers of extremely bright and capable literary scholars and, until recent years, very few first-rate scholars, outside of speech departments, in rhetoric. Now our profession is in difficult circumstances. Many students and the general public perceive us as dilettantes, as members of a college department offering the deadly required writing course and esoteric electives that too seldom tempt students pursuing *real* majors. Our literary sophistication has caused many students who are not English majors to feel that a literary text is a mystery that only the priesthood, which we represent, can interpret. Our practice in the teaching of writing, the work of gifted and exceptional teachers aside, has made many students hate writing because they believe that they will never write well. For these students, writing means acquiring only the skill to write what Ken McCrorie calls "Engfish" and an acceptable level of superficial mechanical correctness. The perception of rhetoric that Fred Newton Scott communicated to his students is by no means widespread; I would guess that more than ninety percent of the teachers in our schools at all levels lack Scott's vision of what rhetoric should be. Thus we face declining enrollments in literature classes, and while writing courses have increased somewhat, we find students taking them for purely practical reasons, not for any exposure to a comprehensive philosophical view of rhetoric in the modern world. I would have to say that, for the most part, we are confronted with a generation of students thoroughly turned off by English as a school subject, taking only as much of it as they have to and swallowing it like bad medicine.

So now we are at the crossroads again. What must we do to restore health and vitality to the profession? Our real mission, as John Gerber pointed out four years ago, has always been the teaching of literacy.[13] We should teach students both to read and to write as well as they can, helping them to improve as much as their capabilities permit. This task applies to marginally competent freshmen as well as to advanced graduate students. And how should we accomplish it? By offering them sensible writing topics, then responding to the substance of *every* student's paper.[14] We must learn to accept the idea that literary texts are more than the classics of our language; they include everything from a seventh grader's paragraph on fishing, to a graduate student's term paper on Chaucer's Pardoner, to *Moby-Dick.* Such a change in attitude will produce a change in priorities; we will become less preoccupied with surface mechanical and grammatical irregularities and more concerned with communication. The benefits to students from this change are tremendous.

In addition, the training of English teachers simply must undergo some transformations. Since most will teach writing as much as they will teach literature, they should be given, at the very least, sufficient background in the rhetorical tradition so that they can understand how present writing courses and their emphases evolved from the past. Instruction in that tradition would begin with Plato's *Gorgias* and *Phaedrus,* Aristotle's *Rhetoric,* Cicero's *De Oratore,* and Quintilian's *Institutes of Rhetoric* and, coming down the centuries, would touch on the major rhetorical documents of each period. In every period of English literature, one can find works on rhetoric that are as important as the literary texts we already know. For example, how many English teachers who have had good eighteenth-century courses read *Tom Jones?* Practically all of them. But how many read Blair's *Lectures on Rhetoric and Belle Lettres* or Campbell's *Philosophy of Rhetoric?* Not very many. My point is that we must graduate future teachers who are as professional in their composition as in their literary training. As Scott said in the prefatory note to "References on the Teaching of Rhetoric and Composition,"

> It [his bibliography] is commended to the attention of those who intend to teach these subjects, and such persons are urged to form a better acquaintance with it; not with the idea that reading about teaching and methods of teaching will bring the power to teach, but with the idea that in this, as in every other line of work, the business of the scholar is to familiarize himself with the literature of his chosen field.[15]

English teachers so prepared and oriented will be able to offer the kind of education students in a democratic society need and can respond to. Perhaps in this way we may teach our students to read, and to write, and to love the study of the English language and literature as they love no other subject.

My questions for modern departments of English, then, are these: (1) whose priorities prevail in your department, those of Francis Child or those of Fred Newton Scott, and (2) if those of Child prevail, can a profession that should aspire to serve the whole spectrum of a university's student body and the larger public from which these young people come fulfill its mission—teaching students at all levels of proficiency and excellence to love reading and writing—with individuals whose interests, competencies, and priorities make them the intellectual descendants of Francis Child? Or, should we now look elsewhere for our professional model, to the man from Michigan who journalist Lee White once called, in a moment of rare levity and affection . . . Great Scott.

Notes

[1] For further discussions of this question see William Riley Parker, "Where Do English Departments Come From?" *College English*, 28 (1967), 339–51; Arthur N. Applebee, *Tradition and Reform in the Teaching of English: A History* (Urbana: National Council of Teachers of English, 1974); and James L. Kinneavy, *A Theory of Discourse* (Englewood Cliffs, N.J.: Prentice-Hall, 1971), pp. 5–13.

[2] See Ronald F. Reid, "The Boylston Professorship of Rhetoric and Oratory, 1806–1904: A Case Study of Changing Concepts of Rhetoric and Pedagogy," *Quarterly Journal of Speech*, 45 (1959), 239–57; Paul E. Ried, "The Boylston Chair of Rhetoric and Oratory," *Western Speech*, 24 (1960), 83–88, and "Francis Child: The Fourth Boylston Professor of Rhetoric and Oratory," *Quarterly Journal of Speech*, 55 (1969), 268–75, and Wallace Douglas, "Rhetoric for the Meritocracy," in Richard Ohmann, *English in America: A Radical View of the Profession* (New York: Oxford Univ. Press, 1976), pp. 97–132.

[3] See Edward T. Channing, *Lectures Read to the Seniors in Harvard College*, ed. Dorothy I. Anderson and Waldo W. Braden, Landmarks in Rhetoric and Public Address (Carbondale: Southern Illinois Univ. Press, 1968), pp. 17–18; Ried, "Francis Child," p. 268.

[4] See Richard M. Weaver, *The Ethics of Rhetoric* (Chicago: Regnery, 1953), pp. 3–27; also, Fred Newton Scott, "Rhetoric Rediviva," ed. Donald C. Stewart, *College Composition and Communication*, 31 (1980), 413–19. Scott is clearly annoyed by the kind of position Channing and, later, Child held: "By one of the most curious perversities in the history of scholarship, Plato has from the earliest times been regarded as rhetoric's uncompromising enemy. . . . Nothing, however, could be farther from the truth. Plato did, indeed, pour out the vials of his scorn upon the rhetoric of his day, but a careful reading of the *Gorgias* and the *Phaedrus* will show that while he castigates the false rhetoric, he holds up in contrast to it the ideal of a true and worthy science" (p. 415).

[5] Sigurd B. Hustvedt, *Ballad Books and Ballad Men* (Cambridge: Harvard Univ. Press, 1930), p. 219. Pp. 241–300 contain the Child-Grundtvig correspondence.

[6] "Ten Years of Harvard," *Harvard Graduates Magazine*, 11 (Sept. 1902), 64; quoted in Reid, p. 250.

[7] *The Fred Newton Scott Anniversary Papers*, ed. Clarence D. Thorpe (Chicago: Univ. of Chicago Press, 1929), pp. 313–19.

8 "Regents Merge Two Departments," *Michigan Alumnus*, 36 (1930), 332. For further testimony to Scott's greatness as a teacher, see Ray Stannard Baker, *Native American* (New York: Scribners, 1941), pp. 252–56; Helen O. Mahin, "Half-Lights," in *The Fred Newton Scott Anniversary Papers*, pp. 1–3; and Jean Paul Slusser, "Recollections of Fred Newton Scott," taped interview, 9 Aug. 1980, Donald Stewart Collection, Michigan Historical Collections, Bentley Historical Library, Univ. of Michigan, Ann Arbor.

9 Letter to Georgia Jackson, 13 Nov. 1916, in the Fred Newton Scott Papers, Michigan Historical Collections, Bentley Historical Library, Univ. of Michigan, Ann Arbor.

10 I might note that a more recent champion of informed attitudes on English usage, Robert C. Pooley of the Univ. of Wisconsin, whose *Teaching English Usage* was a major NCTE publication for years, studied with Leonard and helped complete Leonard's work after his death. Ironically, Pooley was unaware of the Scott connection.

11 Albert R. Kitzhaber, "Rhetoric in American Colleges: 1850–1900," Diss. Univ. of Washington 1953, pp. 114–20.

12 The men of the Michigan rhetoric department, I have discovered from different sources, were very conscious of this phenomenon. As Harvard men came into the English department there and assumed positions of leadership, they looked down on the department of rhetoric and, as Scott grew near retirement, attempted to force the issue of reuniting rhetoric and English. O. J. Campbell was particularly active in this effort, which Michigan's rhetoric professors deeply resented. See the following letters: H. P. Scott to Dean John Effinger, March 1927, in the Michigan University College of Literature, Science, and the Arts Collection, Michigan Historical Collections, Bentley Historical Library, Univ. of Michigan, Ann Arbor; H. P. Scott to F. N. Scott, 26 March 1924; T. E. Rankin to F. N. Scott, 22 June 1926; F. N. Scott to C. C. Little, 1 Dec. 1926; and T. E. Rankin to F. N. Scott, 31 March 1927. The last four are in the Fred Newton Scott Papers. The dispute over amalgamation of rhetoric and English was particularly bitter between Rankin and Campbell. In the 22 June 1926 letter to Scott, Rankin says, "I could not teach well next fall if I were to lend myself to helping to administer this great department into the inferiority which is sure to follow operation of such plans as Mr. Campbell, Mr. Strauss, and Mr. Effinger have proposed in recent months." In the 31 March 1927 letter he refers to Campbell as "unscrupulous through and through" and to Michigan as suffering an era of "Harvardizing and Wisconsinizing and Eastern Boarding-schoolizing." I need hardly point out that Campbell had no more love for Rankin than Rankin had for him. The friction between the easterners, the Harvard men and those they drew to them, and the men who were native to Michigan—particularly the sense of superiority that the Harvard men maintained—is still remembered by A. K. Stevens ("Recollections of Fred Newton Scott," taped interview, 14 Aug. 1980).

13 John Gerber, "Suggestions for a Commonsense Reform of the English Curriculum," *College Composition and Communication*, 28 (1977), 312–16;

see also J. N. Hook, "College English Departments: We May Be Present at Their Birth," *College English*, 40 (1978), 269–73; J. Paul Hunter, "Facing the Eighties," *Profession 80* (New York: MLA, 1980), pp. 1–9; and Paula Johnson, "Writing Programs and the English Department," *Profession 80*, pp. 10–16. For earlier discussions of our methods of teaching English, see Walter Slatoff, *With Respect to Readers* (Ithaca, N.Y.: Cornell Univ. Press, 1970), and Benjamin DeMott, "Last Try," a paper delivered at Seminar to Initiate New Experiments in Undergraduate Instruction, Tufts Univ., 1965; rpt. in John Hawkes, "An Experiment in Teaching Writing to College Freshman," Voice Project (ERIC ED 018 442), pp. 10–12.

[14] Particularly, as this matter applies to novices, see my paper "Acting on the CCCC Language Resolution and Related Matters," *College Composition and Communication*, 31 (1980), 330–32. I might also note how little attention we have paid to our predecessors in this field. For example, the author of one of the most influential rhetoric texts in the nineteenth century told his readers that students of speaking and writing frequently were taught how to do the hardest things, not the easiest, first, a reversal of the normal and sensible pattern of education and then commented on the results such practices produced:

> For it is undeniable that it is much the most difficult to find either propositions to maintain, or arguments to prove them—to know, in short, what to say, or how to say it—on any subject on which one has hardly any information, and no interest; about which he knows little, and cares still less.
>
> Now the subjects usually proposed for School or College exercises are (to the learners themselves) precisely of this description. And hence it commonly happens, that an exercise composed with diligent care by a young student, though it will have cost him far more pains than a *real* letter written by him to his friends, on subjects that interest him, will be very greatly inferior to it. On the *real occasions* of after life (I mean, when the object proposed, is, not to fill up a sheet, a book, or an hour, but to communicate his thoughts, to convince, or persuade),—on these real occasions, for which such exercises were designed to prepare him, he will find that he writes both better, and with more facility, than on the artificial occasion, as it may be called, of composing a Declamation;—that he has been attempting to learn the easier, by practising the harder. (Richard Whately, *Elements of Rhetoric*, 7th ed. [1846], ed. Douglas Ehninger [Carbondale: Southern Illinois Univ. Press, 1963], pp. 21–22)

[15] *Contributions to Rhetorical Theory* (Ann Arbor, [1897]), IV, 1–2.

12

Concepts of Art and the Teaching of Writing

RICHARD E. YOUNG

> ... *glamour* and *grammar* or, in French, *grimoire* and
> *grammaire* were originally the same word and thus com-
> bined, even in the vocabulary, the magical and rationalistic
> aspects of speech.
>
> JACQUELINE DE ROMILLY[1]

I

To understand recent developments in the teaching of writing, we must see them as reactions to an earlier rhetoric. Hence I
would like to begin with a series of statements by the nineteenth-century rhetorician John Genung, whose textbooks, most notably *The
Practical Elements of Rhetoric*, helped establish the paradigm that
has dominated the teaching of rhetoric in the United States for nearly a century. "Rhetoric," he says,

> is literature, taken in its details and impulses, literature in
> the making. . . . it is concerned, as real authorship must be,
> not with a mere grammatical apparatus or with Huxley's log-
> ic engine, but with the whole man, his outfit of conviction
> and emotion, imagination and will, translating himself, as it
> were, into a vital and ordered utterance.[2]

Genung argues, however, that in spite of rhetoric's theoretical concern with the entire process of making literature, any practical treatment of the subject must exclude those acts we would call
creative, particularly those associated with the genesis of the composing process:

> All the work of origination must be left to the writer himself;
> the rhetorical text-book can merely treat of those mental
> habits and powers which give firmness and system to his
> suggestive faculty. . . .[3]

Genung makes a similar point in explaining what he means by "practical rhetoric." Certain rhetorical elements, he says,

> though very real and valuable, are not practical because the ability to employ them cannot be imparted by teaching. They have to exist in the writer himself, in the peculiar bent of his nature. (*Practical Elements*, p. xi)

Since the "work of origination" cannot be taught, he argues, a practical rhetoric must be limited to the conventions and mechanics of discourse—for example, to the modes and structures of discourse, the characteristics of various genres, the norms of style and usage—which are valuable primarily in organizing, editing, and judging what has already been produced by more mysterious powers. "Literature is of course infinitely more than mechanism," he says,

> but in proportion as it becomes more, a text-book of rhetoric has less business with it. It is as mechanism that it must be taught; the rest must be left to the student himself. (*Practical Elements*, p. xii)

For Genung, then, the ability to write with skill requires both a creative gift and a mastery of the craft, but the discipline of rhetoric is of necessity concerned only with craft since only craft can be taught.[4]

By way of contrast, consider this statement by Gordon Rohman, written fifteen years ago, when serious challenges to Genung's position were appearing with increasing frequency:

> Writing is usefully described as a process, something which shows continuous change in time like growth in organic nature. Different things happen at different stages in the process of putting thoughts into words and words onto paper. . . . we divided the process at the point where the "writing idea" is ready for the words and the page: everything before that we called "Pre-Writing," everything after "Writing" and "Re-Writing." . . . what sort of "thinking" precedes writing? By "thinking," we refer to that activity of mind which *brings forth* and develops ideas, plans, designs, not merely the entrance of an idea into one's mind; an active, not a passive enlistment in the "cause" of an idea; conceiving, which includes consecutive logical thinking but much more besides; essentially the imposition of pattern upon experience.[5]

For Genung, rhetoric was a body of information about the forms and norms of competent prose and their uses in the later stages of the composing process—the rhetoric of the finished word. For Rohman, rhetoric does include the craft of writing, but it also includes—and assigns primary importance to—that effort of origination that Genung argued lay beyond the boundaries of a practical rhetoric. "Students," Rohman says, "must learn the structure of thinking that leads to writing since there is no other 'content' to writing apart from the dynamic of conceptualizing" (p. 107).

In these statements by Genung and Rohman we can see the century-old tradition of school rhetoric and what has become the principal argument against it. This argument, which emphasizes the importance of what Rohman calls the "dynamic of conceptualizing" and "creative discovery," is for many the distinctive feature of what is now commonly referred to as the "new rhetoric." W. E. Evans and J. L. Walker describe the difference between the two positions this way:

> While traditional rhetoric was concerned with skill in expressing preconceived arguments and points of view, the new rhetoric is concerned with the exploration of ideas.... The new rhetoric, in short, is based on the notion that the basic process of composition is discovery....[6]

Much of the recent work of rhetoricians has been devoted to finding ways of teaching the process of discovery and of making it a part of a rhetoric that is not only new but practical.

II

Yet the new rhetoric is not nearly so homogenous as this characterization suggests, for we can discern in the developments to which we give that name two apparently irreconcilable positions. And the difference between them is as important theoretically and pedagogically as the difference between the new and the older rhetoric.

Frank D'Angelo has appropriately called one of these positions the "new romanticism."[7] Though we lack the historical studies that would permit us to generalize with confidence, the position seems not so much an innovation in the discipline as a reaffirmation of the vitalist philosophy of an old romanticism enriched by modern psychology. It maintains that the composing process is, or should be, relatively free of deliberate control, that intellect is no better guide to understanding reality than nonlogical processes are, and that the act of composing is a kind of mysterious growth fed by what Henry James called "the deep well of unconscious cerebration."[8] Above all, it insists on the primacy of the imagination in the composing process. "The mystery of language," says James Miller, an advocate of this position,

> is, in large part, the mystery of the processes of the imagination. . . . For too long the assumption has been made that language used by an individual originates in the orderly processes of his rational mind, in his reason, in his faculty of systematic logic. Instruction in language-use has therefore been largely aimed at this logical faculty, in the belief that the teaching of orderly processes will result in good writing. The result, though, has too often been not good writing but dead writing, obedient to all the inhibitions and restraints drilled into the reason, but generally dehumanized and unreadable.[9]

The new romanticism presents the teacher of composition with a difficult problem: that is, how does one teach a mystery? William Coles makes the point well when he says that

> the teaching of writing as writing is the teaching of writing as art. When writing is not taught as art, as more than a craft or a skill, it is not writing that is being taught, but something else. . . . On the other hand, art because it is art, cannot be taught.[10]

Like Genung, Coles believes that the art of composing, as opposed to the craft, cannot be taught; but unlike Genung, he does not on that basis regard a concern with the creative process as impractical: "What is wanted, then, for the teaching of writing as writing, is a way of teaching what cannot be taught, a course to make possible what no course can do" (Coles, p. 111).

The solution to the dilemma is to change the role of the teacher. Teachers are no longer to be purveyors of information about the craft of writing; instead, they must become designers of occasions that stimulate the creative process. Or to put it another way, what Jerome Bruner calls the "expository mode" of teaching is to be replaced by the "hypothetical mode."[11] In contrasting the traditional "classroom of correction" with the new "creative classroom," James Miller says that the latter would be "a place where language would be surrounded not by dogma but by mystery—the mystery of creation. . . ." And, he continues, "the teacher would be free, and would not be telling, but would be exploring with the students alert for the spontaneous, the intuitive, the innovative."[12] Such a situation need not be devoid of rigor, a frequently heard accusation against the new romanticism. For example, Coles establishes a kind of apprentice-master relationship with his students, encouraging them to emulate his own tough-minded intellectual probing and linguistic precision.[13] They learn to be good stylists, in the broadest sense of that term, by observing and trying to imitate the way a good stylist works. If, as the new romantics maintain, the art of writing cannot be taught, the teacher can nevertheless present students with situations in which it can be learned more easily.

The primary disagreement between the new romantics and those representing the second position, whom we might call, for want of a better term, the "new classicists," is a disagreement about what constitutes an art. For the new romantics, art contrasts with craft; the craft of writing refers to skill in technique, or what Genung called "mechanics," a skill that can be taught. Art, however, is associated with more mysterious powers that may be enhanced but that are, finally, unteachable. Art as magic, as glamour.

For the new classicists, art means something quite different: it means the knowledge necessary for producing preconceived results by conscious, directed action. As such, it contrasts not with craft but with knack, that is, a habit acquired through repeated experience. An art, for the new classicist, results from the effort to isolate and generalize what those who have knacks do when they are successful. The distinction is apparent in the opening sentences of Aristotle's *Rhetoric:*

> . . . all men . . . endeavor to criticize or uphold an argument, to defend themselves or accuse. Now, the majority of people do this either at random or with a familiarity arising from habit. But since both these ways are possible, it is clear that matters can be reduced to a system, for it is possible to examine the reason why some attain their end by familiarity and others by chance; and such an examination all would at once admit to be the function of art.[14]

In the *Rhetoric* we find a clear instance of what R. G. Collingwood called the "technical theory of art"—art as grammar.[15]

Aristotle pursues the distinction between knack and art in the *Metaphysics,* where he argues that art arises from experience, emerging as we become aware of the causes of success in carrying out a particular activity. Both those who have a knack and those who have an art can carry out that activity, but, he says, we view artists "as being wiser not in virtue of being able to act, but of having the theory for themselves and knowing the causes."[16]

One crucially important implication of this difference, he

maintains, is that the artist can teach others to carry out the activity, while those who merely have a knack cannot:

> ... it is a sign of the man who knows and of the man who does not know, that the former can teach, and therefore we think art more truly knowledge than experience is; for artists can teach, and men of mere experience cannot. (*Metaphysics* I.a.1; p. 690)

Aristotle is no doubt the most appropriate spokesman for the technical theory of art, but it is apparent today in the work of rhetoricians such as Richard Weaver, Edward Corbett, Richard Hughes, Albert Duhamel, Ross Winterowd, Francis Christensen, and those of us working on tagmemic rhetoric. As this list suggests, one need not be an Aristotelian to embrace the theory.

III

Specifically, what is it that the new classicists teach? The question is worth answering in detail, partly to clarify their conception of art and to dispel misconceptions, which abound, and partly to elaborate on what is in practice a fundamental difference between the two groups of rhetoricians. But a detailed answer also suggests that there may be a basis for accommodation between art as grammar and art as glamour.

What is taught? The answer is, essentially, "heuristics" and whatever is necessary to make them clear and meaningful to the user. Heuristic procedures must not be confused with rule-governed procedures, for if we confuse the two, we tend to reject the use of explicit techniques in composing since few rule-governed procedures are possible in rhetoric. A rule-governed procedure specifies a finite series of steps that can be carried out consciously and mechanically without the aid of intuition or special ability and that if properly carried out always yields a correct result. For example, the procedure for making valid inferences in syllogistic reasoning is rule-governed. But a heuristic procedure provides a series of questions or operations whose results are provisional. Although more or less systematic, a heuristic search is not wholly conscious or mechanical; intuition, relevant knowledge, and skill are also necessary. A heuristic is an explicit strategy for effective guessing. Heuristics are presently available for carrying out many phases of composing, from the formulation of problems to various kinds of editing; some of these procedures are part of our heritage from ancient times, some have been developed within the last twenty years in response to the call for a process-oriented rhetoric.

The use of heuristic procedures implies certain assumptions about the processes they are designed to facilitate. First, their use implies a generic conception of the process. To use a heuristic appropriately writers must see the situation they are confronting at the moment as a specific variant of the *kind* of situation for which the procedure was designed; they must behave as though in some sense they have been there before. If they regard each situation as unique, they have no reason to believe that a technique that was useful once will be useful again. Second, the use of heuristic procedures implies that some, though not necessarily all, phases of the process the writer is trying to control can be carried out deliberately and rationally. That kind of control is a condition for using a heuristic procedure, at least while it is being learned and before it becomes a habitual way of thinking.

If the creative process has generic features, if some of its phases can be consciously directed, and if heuristic procedures can be developed as aids, then it can be taught. To be more precise, certain aspects of the creative process can be taught. We cannot teach direct control of the imaginative act or the unanticipated outcome, but we can teach the heuristics themselves and the appropriate occasions for their use. And this knowledge is important, for heuristic procedures can guide inquiry and stimulate memory and intuition. The imaginative act is not absolutely beyond the writer's control; it can be nourished and encouraged.

These generalizations about heuristics and the technical theory of art become clearer if we recall Francis Christensen's generative rhetoric of the sentence, a technique that uses form to produce ideas.[17] After a close examination of the practice of modern writers who have a knack for good prose—Hemingway, Steinbeck, Faulkner, and others—Christensen identified four principles operating in the production of what he called "cumulative sentences." First, we make a point by adding information to the noun and the verb, which serve as a base from which the meaning will rise. Second, the modifiers usually follow the base clause instead of preceding it or being embedded in it. Third, complexity and precision arise from various levels of generality in the modifiers. Finally, density and richness are the result of the number of modifiers used.

Heuristic procedures enable the writer to bring principles such as these to bear in composing by translating them into questions or operations to be performed. If we were to invent a procedure based on these principles, it might look something like this: study what is being observed, write a base clause about it, and then try piling up at the end of the clause analogies, details, and qualities that serve to refine the original observation. If the writer observes well and has reasonable control of the language and the heuristic—and is lucky—the result can be a sentence like, "He dipped his hands in the bichloride solution and shook them, a quick shake, fingers down, like the fingers of a pianist above the keys" (Christensen, p. 9).

"In composition courses," Christensen says, "we do not really teach our captive charges to write better—we merely *expect* them to. And we do not teach them to write better because we do not know how to teach them to write better" (p. 3). What can we give students if we are interested in having them write elegant and original sentences of this type? One answer is Christensen's four principles and the heuristic derived from them, along with examples, practice, and whatever else is necessary to use them effectively.

Consider another example, from tagmemic rhetoric.[18] The conception of the creative process in tagmemic rhetoric draws heavily on the extensive psychological literature on creativity and problem solving—on the work of Graham Wallas, John Dewey, George Miller, and Leon Festinger in particular. Although the process of original inquiry may seem mysterious and beyond analysis, certain kinds of activity do recur from instance to instance. The process begins with a feeling of difficulty or confusion. If the feeling is insistent, an effort is made to understand its origins, to formulate it as a problem, and to explore data associated with the problem. This exploratory activity often leads to the intuition of one or more possible solutions that are then evaluated for adequacy. If one of these solutions proves adequate, the process is complete; if not, the inquirer may abandon the effort or recycle through various phases of the process. Interspersed are periods of unconscious activity, most notably between the exploration of problematic data and the intuition of possible solutions. Notice that this conception does not insist on the primacy of reason nor does it repudiate nonrational activity; instead it assumes a subtle and elaborate dialectic between the two. In the conscious phases of the process, heuristics can be used—for example, a heuristic can be used for exploring problematic data.

A very young child, when presented with an interesting and enigmatic object, will touch it, taste it, smell it, shake it, and so on—all in an effort to understand it. More mature minds, when confronted with problems, do not abandon physical manipulation but rely more heavily on its intellectual equivalent. We manipulate symbols, instead of things, which immensely increases the range, subtlety, and efficiency of exploration. We compare, contrast, classify, segment, reorder, shift focuses of attention, and so on. By these means, we try to coax intuitions of reasonable solutions.

I am concerned here not only with what we do when engaged in intellectual explorations but also with what we can do to increase our control over it to make it more effective than it might otherwise be. The answer offered by tagmemic rhetoric is a heuristic based on principles of tagmemic linguistics, a linguistic theory developed primarily by Kenneth Pike. These principles, Pike maintains, are universal invariants that underlie all human experience and are characteristic of rationality itself.[19] For example, one such principle states that to describe any unit of experience adequately we must know its contrastive features; otherwise we could not distinguish it from other units. We must also know how it can vary without losing its identity; otherwise we could not recognize it again. And we must know its distribution in various systems, since all units exist in contexts. A knowledge of such contexts enables us to discuss roles; make definitions, predictions, and assumptions about appropriateness of occurrence; and in general perceive the systemic relationships that are part of the unit's identity.

A heuristic exploiting this principle might also ask us to change our mode of perception of the same unit, viewing it as a static, sharply defined particle, as a wave of activity, and as a field of relationships. In each mode we are asked to note the unit's contrastive features, variations, and distributions. In this way we are led through a set of complementary lines of inquiry that direct our attention to features of the unit we might otherwise overlook, help us bring to bear information that we already have in our memories, and identify what we do not yet know. "Discovery," Jerome Bruner observes, ". . . favors the well-prepared mind."[20] The exploratory procedure can be seen as a way of moving the mind out of its habitual grooves, of shaking it loose from a stereotypic past that wants to be retrieved, of helping the writer get beyond the superficial to levels tapped by the romantic's muse.[21]

The great danger of a technical theory of art—of art as grammar—is and has been a tendency to overrationalize the composing process. Techniques tend to multiply beyond utility, and what begins with an effort to develop a teachable art ends with an excessively complex and hence impractical methodology. Whenever writers carry out an activity repeatedly and successfully, it seems possible to generalize about what they are doing and to invent heuristics that enable others to improve their ability to carry out the same activity. In their preoccupation with analysis and method, those holding the theory may ignore our nonrational powers, devising strategies for carrying out processes better dealt with by the unaided mind. But a more adequate understanding of the history of rhetoric and the nature of skillful composing, coupled with careful testing of proposed heuristics for effectiveness, would go far toward curbing unneeded proliferation. Overrationalization is a danger, but it is not an inevitable consequence of the theory.

IV

I have been arguing that two conflicting conceptions of art are discernible in that conglomeration of developments we call the "new rhetoric." The conflict, however, is not new. Jacqueline de Romilly has explored it in the rhetorics of Gorgias, Plato, Aristotle, Longinus, and others; it is clearly apparent in the work of the new rhetoricians of the eighteenth century and romantics like Coleridge in the century that followed. It reemerges every time we think seriously about the discipline. "After all," de Romilly remarks, "it amounts to a struggle between the spell of the irrational and the desire to master it by means of reason. . . ."[22]

The durability of these two fundamental conceptions of rhetorical art and the effectiveness of the pedagogical methods based on them suggest that in some sense both are true, in spite of their seeming incompatibility. We can respond to this conflict by partisan denial of one of the truths, as many have done, though the price of partisanship strikes me as excessively high. Or we can cultivate a Keatsian negative captivity and live with the conflict, exploiting one or the other of the conceptions as it suits our needs as teachers. Such a strategy is not necessarily an evasion of intellectual responsibility; "both-and" may well be, for the moment, a more appropriate response than "either-or." As Niels Bohr once observed, the opposite of a correct statement is an incorrect statement, but the opposite of a deep truth may well be another deep truth.[23] The conflict might well be mitigated if curriculum planners remembered Alfred North Whitehead's argument that education properly moves in a cycle from romantic freedom through an emphasis on precise analysis and intellectual discipline and finally to generalization, the application of principles and techniques to the immediate experiences of life.[24]

Or we can respond by considering the possibility that behind art as glamour and art as grammar there may be a more adequate conception of rhetorical art that does not lead us to affirm the importance of certain psychological powers at the cost of denying the importance of others. If we choose this last course of action, we might begin with a scholarly investigation of the role of heuristic procedures in the rhetorical process, since they call into play both our reason and our imagination.

Notes

[1] Jacqueline de Romilly, *Magic and Rhetoric in Ancient Greece* (Cambridge: Harvard Univ. Press, 1975), p. v.

[2] John Franklin Genung, *The Working Principles of Rhetoric* (Boston: Ginn, 1901), p. vii.

[3] John Franklin Genung, *The Practical Elements of Rhetoric* (Boston: Ginn, 1892), p. 8; hereafter cited in text. Compare Genung's more detailed statement:

> The first stage [of composing], the finding of material by thought or observation, is the fundamental and inclusive office of invention, the distinctive power that we designate in the popular use of the term. Herein lies obviously the heart and center of literary production; it is what the writer finds, in his subject or in the world of thought, that gauges his distinction as an author. Yet this is, of all processes, the one least to be invaded by the rules of the text-book. It is a work so individual, so dependent on the peculiar aptitude and direction of the writer's mind, that each one must be left for the most part to find his way alone, according to the impulse that is in him. (p. 217)

[4] For a discussion of this argument and evidence that it was shared by many of Genung's contemporaries, see Albert Kitzhaber, "Rhetoric in American Colleges: 1850–1900," Diss. Univ. of Washington 1953, pp. 156–67.

[5] D. Gordon Rohman, "Pre-Writing: The Stage of Discovery in the Writing Process," *College Composition and Communication*, 16 (1965), 106; hereafter cited in text.

[6] William H. Evans and Jerry L. Walker, *New Trends in the Teaching of English in Secondary Schools* (Chicago: Rand McNally, 1966), pp. 53–54.

[7] Frank J. D'Angelo, *A Conceptual Theory of Rhetoric* (Cambridge, Mass.: Winthrop, 1975), p. 159.

[8] Henry James, *The Art of the Novel* (New York: Scribners, 1947), pp. 22–23.

[9] James E. Miller, Jr., *Word, Self, Reality: The Rhetoric of Imagination* (New York: Dodd Mead, 1972), pp. 3–4.

[10] W. E. Coles, Jr., "The Teaching of Writing as Writing," *College English*, 29 (1967), 111; hereafter cited in text.

[11] For a discussion of the distinction, see Jerome S. Bruner, *On Knowing: Essays for the Left Hand* (New York: Atheneum, 1965), p. 83.

[12] James E. Miller, Jr., "Everyman with Blue Guitar: Imagination, Creativity, Language," *ADE Bulletin*, No. 43 (Nov. 1974), p. 42.

[13] William E. Coles, Jr., *The Plural I: The Teaching of Writing* (New York: Holt, 1978).

[14] Aristotle, *The "Art" of Rhetoric*, trans. John Henry Freese, Loeb Classical Library (Cambridge: Harvard Univ. Press, 1959), i.i.1–3; p. 3.

[15] R. G. Collingwood, *The Principles of Art* (New York: Oxford Univ. Press, 1958), p. 3.

[16] Aristotle, *Metaphysics*, trans. W. D. Ross, in *The Basic Works of Aristotle*, ed. Richard McKeon (New York: Random, 1941), i.a.1; p. 690.

[17] Francis Christensen, "A Generative Rhetoric of the Sentence," in *Notes*

toward a New Rhetoric: Six Essays for Teachers (New York: Harper, 1967), pp. 1–22.

[18] For a composition text based on the principles of tagmemics, see Richard E. Young, Alton L. Becker, and Kenneth L. Pike, *Rhetoric: Discovery and Change* (New York: Harcourt, 1970).

[19] A convenient summary of the principles can be found in Kenneth L. Pike, "Beyond the Sentence," *College Composition and Communication*, 15 (1964), 129–35.

[20] Bruner, *On Knowing*, p. 82.

[21] For a discussion and illustration of this particular heuristic, see Richard Young, "Methodizing Nature: The Tagmemic Discovery Procedure," *Retrospectives and Perspectives: A Symposium in Rhetoric*, ed. Turner S. Kobler, et al. (Denton: Texas Women's Univ. Press, 1978), pp. 30–39.

[22] de Romilly, *Magic and Rhetoric*, p. 85.

[23] Niels Bohr, "Discussions with Einstein on Epistemological Problems in Atomic Physics," *Atomic Physics and Human Knowledge* (New York: Wiley, 1958). Bohr comments that

in the Institute in Copenhagen, where through those years a number of young physicists from various countries came together for discussions, we used, when in trouble, often to comfort ourselves with jokes, among them the old saying of the two kinds of truth. To the one kind belong statements so simple and clear that the opposite assertion obviously could not be defended. The other kind, the so-called "deep truths," are statements in which the opposite also contains deep truth. Now, the development in a new field will usually pass through stages in which chaos becomes gradually replaced by order; but is not least in the intermediate stage where deep truth prevails that the work is really exciting and inspires the imagination to search for a firmer hold. (p. 66)

[24] Alfred North Whitehead, "The Rhythm of Education" and "The Rhythmic Claims of Freedom and Discipline," *The Aims of Education and Other Essays* (New York: Free Press, 1967).

Index

Aberdeen, University of, 95
Academic history, 8
Adams, John Quincy, 4
ADE Bulletin, 18n
Aesthetic, 24–25
Affective force of discourse, 109
Affective realm versus cognitive realm, 78
Agreement (property of mind), 97–98
Alienation of rhetoric from the humanities, 19–20, 23
Analysis, 110, 116n; of written texts, 53
Anthropismos, 20
Anti-Ciceronians, 23
Antirhetoricians of the Royal Society, 23
Antiutilitarian literary elite, 14
Argument, 117n
Aristippus, 20
Aristotle, vii, 5, 7, 22, 32, 50, 62, 66–67, 78–79, 95, 97, 99–101, 139; analysis of emotion, 76; authority of, 65; definition of rhetoric, 70; and invention, 31; *Metaphysics*, 134–35, 140n; *Rhetoric*, v, 31–32, 45n, 52, 71n, 80, 82, 115n, 126, 134, 140n
Arnold, Matthew, 16
Arrangement, 50, 117n; argumentative, 113
Ars dictaminis (craft of letter writing), 115n
Ars poetica (skill of application of figures and tropes to poetry), 115n
Ars praedicandi (art of preaching), 115n
Art: distinguished from knack, 134; as glamour, 139; as grammar, 134–35, 138, 139; as magic, 134–35; as rhetoric, 114n; of writing, 113, 134
Artist as teacher, 135
Ascham, Roger, 5
Assignments: in degrees of difficulty, 90–91; sequenced, 90
Associationist principles of epistemology, 96
Association psychology, v, 95–96, 102, 106; and figures of speech, 98; and persuasion, 99–100
Augustine, *On Christian Doctrine*, 114–15n
Autotutorial electronics, vi, 11
Aytoun, William Edmonstone, 86

Back to basics, 111–13
Bacon, Francis, 51, 64, 67, 75, 121
Bain, Alexander, 53, 95; *Autobiography*, 96, 103n; *Emotions and the Will*, 96, 100, 103n; *English Composition and*

Rhetoric, v, 56n, 95–104, 116n; figures of speech, 104n; and mind of reader, 102; psychological research, 96; psychology of volition, 100–01; *Senses and the Intellect*, 96–99, 103n; "shock of recognition," 98; theory of pleasure and pain, 101–02
Basics, 47, 54, 56
Becker, Alton L., 116n, 141n
Belles lettres movement, 15, 107; curriculum, 106
Belletristic rhetorics, 115n; literature, 23
Blair, Hugh, 15, 53; *Lectures on Rhetoric and Belles Lettres*, 106, 109, 115n, 126
Bohr, Niels, 141n
Booth, Wayne, 105; *Modern Dogma and the Rhetoric of Assent*, 115n
Boyle, Robert, 75
Boylston Professorship, Harvard University, 4, 119–20, 127n
Bracciolini, Poggio, 5
Britton, James, 113
Burke, Kenneth, 105; concept of identification, 77; *Counter-Statement*, 71n; notion of form, 61; *Rhetoric of Motives*, 83n, 115n

Cambridge University, 6
Campbell, George, 53, 75; *Philosophy of Rhetoric*, 78, 83n, 106, 115n, 126
Chairs of English literature, 86
Channing, Edward T., 4, 119; *Lectures Read to the Seniors at Harvard College*, 127n
Child, Francis James, vi, 4, 86, 119–22, 125–27; *English and Scottish Popular Ballads*, 120
Cicero, Marcus Tullius, vi, 6, 21, 25, 49, 58, 61–62, 64, 70, 75; as critic of Socrates, 3, 62; *De Inventione*, 22, 63; *De Oratore*, 3, 11n, 48, 57n, 62, 115n, 126; *Orator*, 62, 71n; on plain style, 60, 63; and Quintilian, 58; *Rhetorica ad Herrenium*, 20; rhetorical theory, 60; six-part form, 80
Clarity, 56, 66
Clark, Donald Lemen, 25; *John Milton at St. Paul's School*, 57n; *Rhetoric in Greco-Roman Education*, 27n, 57n
Class size problem, 90
Climax, 11n
Cognitive-developmental approach, 102
Cognitive process: in Locke, 76
Cognitive psychology, v
Coles, William E., Jr., 133; *The Plural I: The Teaching of Writing*, 42, 45n, 140n

College Board, 17
"Colours of *Rhetorick*," 65
Communication, 58–59, 105, 109;
    function, 108; as goal, 126; paradigm
    for rhetorical education, 110; purpose,
    110, 115n
Comparison and contrast, 110, 116n
Compassion, 21
Composing process, 132, 138
Composition, 9, 13, 16–17, 50, 55, 109;
    courses, 14, 75, 121, 124, 137; in
    curriculum, 112; exercises in, 10, 22,
    25, 49, 53–54; imagination in, 133; as
    instruction in form, 54, 112; and
    literature, 121; vs. literature, 8; oral,
    4; problem of, 13; research in, 102; as
    rhetoric, 124; staff for 8. *See also
    Progymnasmata*; Rhetoric; Writing
Comprehensibility: criteria, 59
Comprehensibility Assurance Test, 59
Conference on College Composition and
    Communication, 14
Contiguity, principle of, 97
Contrast, principle of, 97
Controversy, 22
Corbett, Edward P. J., v, 73–84, 135;
    *Classical Rhetoric for the Modern
    Student*, 57n, 72n
Cornell University, 16, 54; department of
    speech, 52
Correctness, rules of, 113–14
Craft (of writing), 131–34
"Creative classroom," 133
Creative gift, 131
Creative intentionality, 53
Creative process, as teachable, 136
Creative writing, 13, 24; faculty, 8
Creativity, 6; vs. mechanism, vii
Criticism of literature, 4
Cultural bias of intelligence tests, 77
Curricular courage, vi, 3, 8, 10
Curriculum, 4, 7, 10, 24–25, 46; classical,
    121; of Whately-Blair, 111

D'Angelo, Frank J., 99, 132; *Conceptual
    Theory of Rhetoric*, 104n, 140n
Day, Henry, v, 106, 109–10, 113;
    Elements of the Art of Rhetoric, 108,
    111, 116n
Debate, 50
Declamatio, 6, 120
Deduction vs. induction, 78–79
Degrees: of assent, 80; of assignment
    difficulty, 90; of certainty, 79
Delivery, 50–51
Demonstration, 79
Demosthenes, 70
Departmentalization of disciplines, 23
Departments: of English, 3, 8, 10, 16,
    23–25, 118, 121; of speech, Cornell, 52;
    of speech communications, 25; of
    linguistics, 52
de Romilly, Jacqueline, 139; *Magic and
    Rhetoric in Ancient Greece*, 140n,141n

Descartes, René, 65–66, 75
Description, 110, 116n
Dialectic, 32, 38, 49–50; and rhetoric, 31,
    36
Dialogue, 35, 108
Diogenes, Laertius, *Lives of the
    Philosophers*, 26n
Discovery, as basic process of
    composition, 132
Discrimination (property of mind), 97–98
Discussion hours, 89–90
Disputatiousness of rhetoricians, 65
Document Design Center, Carnegie-
    Mellon University, 58
Dowden, Edward, 15–17
Dramatistic presentation, 32
Dryden, John, 73
Duffey, Joseph, 111–12

Edinburgh, Univeristy of, 15, 85–94
Education, 21–23; classical, 54, 85;
    democratic mode of, 85–86; elitist, 15;
    in literacy, 56; state departments of,
    24
Eighteenth century, 102, 139; issues in
    rhetoric, 73–82
Elective courses in composition, 121
Elective system, 4
Eleutheria, 20
Elocution, 116n, 117n
Elocutionary movement, 52, 107, 115n
Eloquence, 36, 49, 56, 81, 107; and
    imitation, 70; and wisdom, 63
Eloquence a Virtue. See Theremin,
    Franz
Elyot, Sir Thomas, 5
Emig, Janet, 113, 117n
Emotional appeal, 100, 102, 116n
Emotion as influence on will, 101
Emotions and the Will, The. See Bain,
    Alexander
Emotions of audience, 25; in Aristotle,
    76
Empirically verifiable objectivity, 51
Empirically verified data, 80
Empiricism, 9, 64, 76
Engaged prose, 24
English as profession, 118–19, 125
English departments, vi, 3, 8, 10, 16,
    23–25, 118; and speech departments,
    121; and study of literature, 121
English literature, 86, 89, 124
English teachers, 13–14, 58, 126
Enthymeme (rhetorical proof), 80
Entrance examinations, 94
Epistemology, 73
Erasmus, Desiderius, *De Copia*, 115n
Erickson, Keith V., 12n
Essayists, exclusion of, 24
Ethics, 36, 39, 100, 102, 105, 107; of
    audience, 107, 116n; of rhetoric, 33
Euripides, *Medea*, 22
Example, as rhetorical proof, 80
Excitation, 116n

Exemplification, 110
Exercises in composition, 49, 54, 68, 69.
  See also Progymnasmata
Explanatory discourse, 116n
Exposition, 53, 74; five processes in, 110,
  116n
Expository writing, 75; in science, 24–25;
  urged by Day, 109

Facilitas, 6–7
Fallacies, formal and material, 79
Fallible proofs, 80
Fénelon, Jacques, *Dialogues sur
  l'éloquence*, 81
Figures: of antithesis, 98; and
  association psychology, 98; of
  contiguity, 98; of contrast, 99; as
  natural operations of mind, 98;
  opposed by Locke, 81; of speech, 60,
  62–63, 70, 96–97, 102
Flesch, Rudolf, 59; *Art of Readable
  Writing*, 82
Fontenelle, Bernard Le Bouvier de,
  65–66
Forensics (the art of gesture), 52
Form, 32, 65, 68
Form recognition, 6
Frankfurt school, 26
Free speech, 21

Genung, John, *Practical Elements of
  Rhetoric*, vii, 130–34, 140n
Geoffrey of Vinsauf, 61; *Poetria Nova*,
  71n
Geometry as general method, 66
German scholarship, 4
Gibson, Walker, 59; *Tough, Sweet and
  Stuffy*, 71n
Glasgow, University of, 85–94
Gorgias, vii, 139
Gorgias. See Plato
Grammar, 7, 20, 48–49; definition of, 7
Grammar school, 48
Grammaticus, 48–49
Guthrie, Warren, "Development of
  Rhetorical Theory in America," 115n

Hadas, Moses, *Humanism: The Greek
  Ideal and Its Survival*, 27n
Halloran, S. Michael, vi, 58–72
Harvard College, 12n
Harvardization of English departments,
  vi, 118–29
Harvard University, 4–5, 11, 86, 119–20,
  128n; English department, 121–22;
  philosophy of composition teaching,
  124; rhetoric program, 124
Heuristics, vii, 76–77, 135–36, 139
High schools: and elementary schools,
  19; and journalism courses, 24
Hill, Adams Sherman, 4
Hirsch, E. D., Jr., vi, 13–18, 59;
  Philosophy of Composition, 71n, 83n,
  112, 117n; "relative readability," 75

Historical linguistics, 52
History: American, 11; and literature,
  21; need for understanding rhetorical
  history, v–vi, 3–5, 7, 11, 14, 19–20, 48,
  60, 69, 73–74, 82, 85–86, 95, 103, 105,
  118–19, 130, 138; of paragraph, 103
Holistic approaches, 67
Homer, *Iliad, Odyssey*, 25, 27n
Hope, Matthew, v, 106, 110–13;
  Princeton Textbook in Rhetoric, 106,
  110, 116n, 117n
Horner, Winifred B., v, 85–94;
  Historical Rhetoric, 11n
Howell, Wilbur S., v, 74; *Eighteenth-
  Century British Logic and Rhetoric*,
  83–84n
Hughes, Richard, 135
Hughes, Thomas, *Tom Brown's School
  Days*, 12n
Humanism, vi
Humanist alternative, 105
Humanistic approach to teaching
  writing, 111–12
Humanistic perspective, 105–06, 113
Humanitas, 20
Humanities, 19–28
Humanities in American Life, The, vi,
  19, 26n
Hume, David, "Of Eloquence," 78

Ideas: dependent on experiences, 77
Illiteracy, 47
Imitation, 4, 6–7, 70
Impassioned prose, 25
Impersonality as stylistic ideal, 65,
  67–68
Individual student populations, 117n
Induction vs. deduction, 78–79
Instruction by example, 82
Integration, 9
Intelligibility as mechanism, 66
Interpersonal nature of discourse, 109
Introduction, 80
Intuition, 79, 135, 137
Invention, 50, 108–09, 116n, 117n; of
  arguments, 31; and arrangement in
  compositions, 49; central to
  composition, 110; procedures, 110
Inventive topoi, 53
Irony, 40
Isocrates, 21, 25, 63; "Antidosis," 27n,
  72; father of humanism, 21;
  Panegyricus, 22, 27n; power of
  speech, 63
Ivy League, 16

Jaeger, Werner, *Paideia*, 27n
James, Henry, 132
Jardine, George, v, 87, 89–94; *Outlines
  of Philosophical Education*, 88–89,94n
Jefferson, Thomas, 9
Jeffrey, Francis, 87
John of Garland, 61; *De Arte Prosayca,
  Metrica, et Rithmica*, 71n

Johns Hopkins University, 4, 119
Johnson, Nan, v, 105–17
Johnson, Samuel, 87
Jones, Richard Foster, 64
Journalism, 13, 24, 123
Judgment (as faculty), 79

Kennedy, George A., 11n; *Art of Persuasion in Greece*, 71n
Kierkegaard, Søren, 24, 26, 27–28n
Kinds of discourse, 37
Kinneavy, James L., vi, 19–28, 110; *Theory of Discourse*, 116n, 127n
Kittredge, George Lyman, 120, 122
Kitzhaber, Albert Raymond, 123–24; "Rhetoric in American Colleges 1850–1900," 104n, 128n, 140n
Knowledge through experience, 76

Language, 23; competence, 113; coordinated teaching of, 5; and culture, 77; as instrument of communication, 75; and literacy, 15; and literature, 23; skills and society, 112; as social phenomenon, 123
Lanham, Richard, 68
Lectures, 85, 87, 89; in English, 88
Lewis, Edwin Herbert, *History of the English Paragraph*, 103n
Liberal arts, 20, 22–23, 85, 94, 116n; vs. specialization, 85
Liberal education vs. professional preparation, 23
Lincoln, Abraham, 9
Linguistic ability, 6, 133
Listening, 6, 11
Literacy, 10, 52; crisis, 13, 47; and democracy, 56; and literature, 14–16, 18; maintenance, 114; mass, 15; as skill development, 112
Literary: faculty, 8; studies, 14, 16, 49
Literator, 48
Literature, 7, 10–11, 113; classes, 125; and composition, 7; at Harvard, 124; and language, 23; and literacy, 14–16, 18; and rhetoric, 125
Locke, John, 73–84; "Abuse of Words," 75; attack on syllogism, 78; *An Essay concerning Human Understanding*, v, 73–74, 82–83; opposed to figurative language, 81. *See also* MacLean, Kenneth
Logic, 20, 23, 52, 73, 78, 87, 113, 115n, 131; and rhetoric, 51
Logical appeals, 31
Longinus, vii, 139
Lysias, 33–34, 36, 39

MacLean, Kenneth, *John Locke and English Literature of the Eighteenth Century*, 73
MacLeish, Archibald, 5
Manner, 114
Manual. See Bain, Alexander

Marcuse, Herbert, *One-Dimensional Man*, 28n
Marrou, Henri I., *History of Education in Antiquity*, 27n
Mastery of craft, 131
Mathematics, 66, 96; at Cambridge, 87; in communication, 59; as model for scientific inquiry, 78
McLuhan, Marshall, 9
Media, 25
Memorization, 4, 6, 49, 106, 113
Memory, 9, 50–51, 90
Mental properties, in Bain, 97–98
Metaphor, 60, 62
Methods of teaching, 126
Michigan, University of, 122, 124; rhetoric department, 128n
Microprocessor, vi, 11
Milic, Louis, 62, 68, 72n
Miller, Perry, 81, 84; *New England Mind*, 71–72n
Miller, Susan, v–vi, 46–57
Milton, John, 6, 12n
Minimal-competency tests, 17
Minority students, 26
Moral philosophy, 87, 96
Motivation, professional, 13–14, 17
Mulder, John, *Temple of the Mind*, 68
Mulderig, Gerald, v, 95–104
Murphy, James J., vi, 3–12; *Quintilian on the Early Education of the Citizen-Orator*, 12n; *Renaissance Rhetoric: A Short-Title Catalog*, 12n; *Rhetoric in the Middle Ages*, 57n, 71n
Murray, Donald, 113

Narration, 80, 110, 116n
National Council of the Teachers of English (NCTE), 46, 52; 1914 convention, 23
Natural philosophy, 87
New classicism, vii, 134–35; vs. new romanticism, 135
New Criticism, 24, 53
Newman, Edwin, 58
Newman, John Henry, 16, 23–24, 80; *Essay in Aid of a Grammar of Assent*, 74, 84n; *Idea of a University*, 22, 27n
New rhetoric, vii, 108, 132, 139
New romanticism, vii, 132–35; vs. new classicism, 135
Newton, Isaac, 75, 86
New York Regent's National Advisory Committee, 17
New York State, 17
Nicolson, Marjorie, *Science and Imagination*, 67, 72n

Ohio State University, 52
Ohmann, Richard, *English in America: A Radical View of the Profession*, 42, 45n
Oral composition, 4

Orality, 9–10
Oratory, 4, 25, 36; as communicative, 114n; and composition, 120; distrust of, 119; as sophistic, 119–20
"Origination," 130–32
Ornamentation, 51, 60, 62
Ornate vs. plain style, 81–82
Oxford University, 12, 52

Paideia, 22
Panhellenism, 21–22
Paradigmatic studies of written discourse, 53
Paragraph: Day's four modes of development, 110; history of, 103n; "rules" for writing, 95
Parallel structures, 11
Paraphrase, as exercise, 6, 49, 90
Parsing, 49
Partition, 80
Patterns of organization, without purpose, 53
Patton, John H., 77–78, 83n
Peer evaluation, 93
Peitho, 26
Peroration, 80
Personalized computer manuals, 67
Persuasion, 20, 23–25, 31, 37, 49, 53, 62, 74, 75, 106–07, 115n, 116n; by argument, 100; and association psychology, 99; audience identification in, 107; by emotional appeals, 96, 100–01; as ethical art, 110–11; vs. exposition in Day's theory, 110; not formulaic, 107; inventional procedures for, 110; values in, 107
Ph.D. program, 16
Phaedrus. See Plato
Philanthropia, 20
Philology, 23, 52
Philosopher, 36–37, 63
Philosophical aims of rhetoric, 116n
Philosophy and rhetoric as distinct, 63
Piaget, Jean, 76
Pike, Kenneth L., 116n, 138, 141n
Pisteis (rhetorical proofs), 80
Plain English, 58
Plain language, vi, 58–59, 71; as "plain style," 60
Plain style, vi, 58, 60, 81; among Puritans, 71–72n; for scientific discourse, 61, 64. *See also* Style
Plato, vii, 22, 120, 139; *Gorgias*, 22, 115n, 119, 127n; *Meno*, 22; *Phaedrus*, v, 31–45, 119, 126, 127n; soul as charioteer, 36–37
Platonic method, 49
Polanyi, Michael, *Personal Knowledge*, 45n, 70, 72n
Positivism, vi, 9, 60
Postman, Neal, 9
Power of speech, 27n
Practical Elements of Rhetoric, The. See Genung, John

Practical humanism, 22
Pragmatic model of writing, 55
Prewriting, 91, 131
Princeton Textbook, The. See Hope, Matthew
Prizes for themes, 93
Probabilities vs. certainties, 79–80
Process-oriented rhetoric, 135
Programmatic approach, 10
Progymnasmata, or elementary composition exercises, 10, 22, 25, 49, 53. *See also* Composition
Proofs, inartistic, 76
Propriety, as virtue of style, 61
Prose rhythm, 60
Protagoras, 21
Psychology, 73, 96, 102; of assent, 80; and emotion, 102; experimental, 123; and figures of speech, 99; in nineteenth century, 95; and volition, 102. *See also* Association psychology; Cognitive psychology
Puritan commitment to plain style, 61, 71–72n

Quantification of communication, impossibility of, 70–71
Quintilian, Marcus Fabius, vi, 4, 6, 10, 49, 56; bibliography of, 12n; *Institutes of Oratory*, 5, 12, 48, 57n, 115n, 126
Quiz on lecture, 90

Ramus, Peter, 32, 51; *Dialectic*, 115n; theory of rhetoric as ornament, 115n
Readability: as "communicative writing," 117n; vs. maturity, 69; measure of, 60; relative, 75
Reading, 4, 8–9; and writing, 3, 11, 125, 127
Readings in Classical Rhetoric, 72n
Reason: and communication, 91; and imagination, 51, 139
Recitation, 6, 91
Refutation, 80, 117n
Research first, literature second, 124
Research in literacy, 17
Retentiveness (property of mind), 97–98
Rhapsodes, 41
Rhetor, 48–49
Rhetoric, 22, 23, 25, 32–33, 38–39, 42, 49, 51, 63, 75, 87–88, 107, 109, 113, 135; American attitude toward, 5; as analysis of discourse, 25; as art of arrangement, 36; and belles lettres, 15, 88, 111; as body of information, 131; canons of, 50; classical and Renaissance, 55, 69; competence in, 50; component of humanism, 24; as composition, 124; conceptual theory of, 99, 104n, 140n; definition of, 109, 111; as democratic education, 93–94; devices of, 66–67, 69; distinct from philosophy, 63; in eighteenth century, 73–82; as ethical force, 107;

generative, vii, 136, 140n; at Harvard, 124; as heart of liberal education, 94; in high school, 26; as instruction in grammar and mechanics, 124; not a knack or a style, 107; as literature, 130; need for understanding history, v–vi, 3–5, 7, 11, 14, 19–20, 48, 60, 69, 73–74, 82, 85–86, 95, 103, 105, 118–19, 130, 138; in nineteenth century, 114, 129n, 130; as persuasion by speech, 21; philosophic basis of, 106; proof in, 78, 80; relation to other disciplines, 123; as skill of argumentation, 109; as skills management, 105; as socially responsible, 111; as style, 66–67, 69, 109; textbook for, 130–31; in textbooks, 53; as theory of communication, 94, 113, 115n; topics of invention, 53; tradition of, vii, 9, 33, 69, 126

Rhetoric, The. See Aristotle

Rhetorical education, 25, 106, 109, 111, 115n, 123; in nineteenth century, 114

Rhetorica ad Herrenium. See Cicero

Right rhetoric, 36–37

Romanticism, 132

Royal Society, 65, 81; and scientific style, 75. *See also* Sprat, Thomas

Safire, William, 58

St. Andrews, University of, 85

St. Paul's School, London, 12n

Sale, William, 16

Schemes and tropes, 69, 81. *See also* Style

Scholars in literacy, 17

Scholastics, 65

Science, 58, 63, 88; attack on systems, 70; of philology, 15

Scientific method, 64, 67

Scientific revolution, 64

Scott, Fred Newton, vi, 119, 122–27; *Contributions to Rhetorical Theory*, 129n; system of rhetoric, 123

Scottish universities, v, 85–94

Self-expression, 109

Semantic adequacy, 117n

Semiological approach to literature, 24

Sensation, 79

Senses and the Intellect, The. See Bain, Alexander

Separation: of linguistic form and content, 112; of reading from writing, 7; of writing from literature, vi

Sequence of instruction, 46

Shakespeare, William, 6, 12n, 15, 57n, 121

Shaughnessy, Mina: communicative perspective, 114; *Errors and Expectations*, 113, 117n

Shedd, William, 106

Sheridan, Thomas, *Lectures on Elocution*, 115n

"Shock of recognition." *See* Bain, Alexander

Sight, sound, and sense, 6

Similarity, principle of, 97

Skills management as rhetoric, 105

Skills-oriented writing classes, 112

Smith, Adam, *Lectures on Rhetoric and Belles Lettres*, 81, 88

Social impact of language competence, 112

Socrates, 3, 33–34, 36, 38–42

Socratic dialogue, 33

Sophists, 21

Speaking, 4, 6; exercises (oral composition), 11; and writing, 129n

Speech and elocution, vi, 23

Speech and writing: relative worth, 36; speech as inferior, 121

Speech departments, vii, 10, 125; new, 23

Speeches, 22–23

Split between form and content, 65, 68

Sprat, Thomas, 65; *History of the Royal Society*, 72n, 81

Standards for writing, 56

Status, doctrine of, 48

Steinhoff, Virginia N., v, 31–45

Stewart, Donald C., vi, 11n, 118–29

Strategies of organization and argument, 69

Students as "examiners," 93

Student voices, as part of culture, 113

Study: of communication, 67; of literature, 15, 112, 120; of literature as opposed to rhetoric, 119

Style, 50, 96, 113, 116n, 117n; in Aristotle, 61; as calculus of personality, 68–69; in Cicero, 60–61, 63, 69; excessive attention to, 108; as matter of genre, 61; plain versus ornate, 81–82; and scientific method, 64; split between form and content, 65, 68; three levels with three effects, 61

Stylistics, 51, 55, 59, 110

Symbols, 137

Sympathy, appeal to, 101

Systematic rhetorics, 111

Tabula rasa of consciousness, 76

Tacitus, 26

Tagmemic rhetoric, vii, 137–38

Teachers: of composition, 9–10, 56, 76; of creativity, 133; of English, vii, 73; of writing, 32, 82, 90

Teaching: American, 7; of analysis, 25; assistants, 11; of composition, 80; of literacy, 125; of writing, 16–17, 54, 112, 130, 133

Technical writing, 13

Techniques, 69, 106, 136

Texas Council for the Humanities, 24

Textbooks: of composition, 15; of rhetoric, 53, 130–31

Themes: choosing own topics, 92; four orders of, 91–92; overlooking faults, 93; prizes for, 93; read aloud, 93;

reading and evaluation, 90; time wasted correcting, 120; varied subjects, 92
Theoria and *praxis*, 22
Theorists, contemporary Platonic, 42
Theory of discourse, 42
Theremin, Franz, v, 105–11, 113, 116n; *Eloquence a Virtue*, 106, 108, 111, 115n
Theuth (inventor of writing), 38
Thinking the unthinkable, 10
Topics, 76
Topic sentence, 95
Toulmin, Stephen, 79
Trivium, 49–50
Truth, central function of discourse, 106
Tutorial system, 89

University subjects, 120

Vergil, *Bucolics*, 61
Vernacular literature, 15
Virginia, University of, 14
Volition, 102

Weaver, Richard M., 31–33, 115n, 135; *Ethics of Rhetoric*, 45n, 127n; "Language Is Sermonic," 115n
Whately, Richard, 53, 111; definition of rhetoric as persuasion, 111; *Elements of Rhetoric*, 106, 109, 115n, 129n; *Logic*, 4
Whitburn, Merrill D., vi, 58–72
Wilson, Thomas, *Art of Rhetoric*, 115n
Winterowd, W. Ross, 110, 135; *Contemporary Writer*, 116n
Wisconsin, University of, at Milwaukee, 55
Word-processing technology, 59
Word processor, 8
Wordsworth, William, "Immortality Ode," 76
Wotton, William, *Reflections upon Ancient and Modern Learning*, 64, 66, 72n
Writing, 3, 6, 8–9, 11, 38, 87; advanced, 13; argumentative, 75; assignments, 49, 53–55, 68–69, 77, 90–93; classes, 13, 16, 125; as communication process, 113; limitations, 41; as mechanical correctness, 125; as practical subject, 113; as process, 91, 131; and reading, 11, 125, 127; skills, 13, 111; as socially valuable, 114; tests, 17
Written speech, 33

Yale University: doctoral program, 16–17; English department, 13–18
Young, Richard E., vii, 104n, 110, 116n, 130–41